CONCILIUM
ADVISORY COMMITTEE

Gregory Baum	Montreal/QC. Canada
José Oscar Beozzo	São Paulo, SP Brazil
Wim Beuken	Louvain, Belgium
Leonardo Boff	Petrópolis, Brazil
John Coleman	Los Angeles, CA. USA
Norbert Greinacher	Tübingen, Germany
Gustavo Gutiérrez	Lima, Peru
Hermann Häring	Tübingen, Germany
Werner G. Jeanrond	Oslo, Norway
Jean-Pierre Jossua	Paris, France
Maureen Junker-Kenny	Dublin, Ireland
François Kabasele Lumbala	Kinshasa, Rep. Dem. Congo
Nicholas Lash	Cambridge, UK
Mary-John Mananzan	Manila, The Philippines
Alberto Melloni	Reggio, Emilia Italy
Norbert Mette	Münster, Germany
Dietmar Mieth	Tübingen, Germany
Jürgen Moltmann	Tübingen, Germany
Teresa Okure	Port Harcourt, Nigeria
Aloysius Pieris	Kelaniya/Colombo, Sri Lanka
Giuseppe Ruggieri	Catania, Italy
Paul Schotsmans	Louvain, Belgium
Janet Martin Soskice	Cambridge, UK
Elsa Tamez	San José, Costa Rica
Christoph Theobald	Paris, France
David Tracy	Chicago, Ill. USA
Marciano Vidal	Madrid, Spain
Ellen van Wolde	Tilburg, The Netherlands
Johannes Zizioulas	Pergamo, Turkey
Regina Ammicht Quinn	Tübingen Germany
Hille Haker	Chicago, USA
Jon Sobrino	San Salvador, El Salvador
Luiz Carlos Susin	Porto Alegre, Brazil
Silvia Scatena	Bologna, Italy
Susan A. Ross	USA, Los Angeles
Solange Lefebvre	Montreal/QC. Canada
Erik Borgman	Amsterdam, Netherlands
Andres Torres Queiruga	Santiago, Spain

CONCILIUM 2020/4

Signs of Hope in Muslim-Christian Relations

Edited by

Catherine Cornille, Daniel Franklin Pilario,
Mile Babic

Published in 2020 by SCM Press, 3rd Floor, Invicta House, 108–114 Golden Lane, London EC1Y 0TG.

SCM Press is an imprint of Hymns Ancient & Modern Ltd (a registered charity) 13A Hellesdon Park Road, Norwich NR6 5DR, UK

Copyright © International Association of Conciliar Theology, Madras (India)

www.concilium.in

English translations copyright © 2020 Hymns Ancient & Modern Ltd.

All rights reserved. No part of this publication may be reproduced, stored in a retrieval system, or transmitted, in any form or by any means, electronic, mechanical, photocopying or otherwise, without the prior written permission of the Board of Directors of Concilium.

ISBN 978-0-334-05959-2

Concilium is published in March, June, August, October, December

Contents

Editorial   7

Part One: Official Statements and Documents

Nostra Aetate and Encounters of Friendship   13
WILHELMUS VALKENBERG

A Common Word between Us and You – a Carrier of Hope   22
VEBJØRN L. HORSFJORD

Migration as a Kairos Moment for Protestant-Muslim Dialogue   34
JOSHUA RALSTON

Part Two: Hope in Sacrifice and Solidarity

Monastic-Muslim Dialogue   47
WILLIAM SKUDLAREK

Martyrdom and Hope in Muslim-Christian Dialogue   56
CHRISTIAN S. KROKUS

Part Three: Signs of Hope in Different Parts of the World

Signs of Hope for Christian-Muslim Relations in Indonesia   69
ALBERTUS BAGUS LAKSANA, S.J.

Academic Collaboration in Germany   77
KLAUS VON STOSCH

The Dialogue School in Belgium   84
LAURIE JOHNSTON

Grassroots Initiatives in Turkey   92
CLAUDIO MONGE, OP

Collaboration for Peace in Nigeria   99
MARINUS CHIJIOKE IWUCHUKWU

Hospitality and Mutuality in Egypt   107
JEAN DRUEL

Part Four: Hope for the Future of Muslim-Christian Relations

A Shared Desire for a Universal Vision   117
DANIEL A. MADIGAN, S.J.

A Shared Culture of Justice and Reconciliation   127
ASMA AFSARUDDIN

Part Five: Theological Forum - Public Theology in the Digital Age

Who Participates in the Digital Theological Conversation?   141
STEPHEN OKEY

Millennials and Public Theology in a Digital Age   147
KATHERINE G. SCHMIDT

Contributors   153

Editorial

Even though, or because Islam is historically and theologically closely related to Christianity, the relationship between these two religions is generally depicted in terms of their disagreements, tensions and conflicts. From the crusades to the current war against terrorism, the main focus has been on the seemingly irreconcilable theological differences between the two religions and on their inevitable social and political discord. It has been further fuelled by the 'clash of civilizations' discourse which has gained broad purchase since the end of the twentieth century This dominant narrative may lead to a certain desperation and hopelessness with regard to the possibility for peaceful or harmonious coexistence and mutually enriching dialogue between the two religions. It is therefore important to counter this narrative with stories of figures, events, movements, or practices that exemplify genuine love and respect for the religious other, mutual learning, and commitment to a higher common good.

There are examples of such stories throughout history, from the Indian emperor Akbar (1542-1605) to the French scholar Louis Massignon (1883-1962), and from the period of Convivencia in medieval Spain to the relatively peaceful coexistence of Muslims and Christians in Indonesia. Many individuals and groups are currently involved in various types of constructive dialogue through social projects, theological exchange, and visionary pursuits. It is important to call attention to these projects in order to draw hope and inspiration for the future of Muslim-Christian relations.

This issue of *Concilium* focuses on recent and current developments in Muslim-Christian relations. Part I discusses statements made by official representatives of the two traditions, the Vatican II declaration *Nostra Aetate* and papal actions and statements on the Christian side, and the 2007 document *A Common Word Between Us and You* on the Muslim side. These texts demonstrate the growing friendship on the part of official representatives of both traditions, and a genuine desire to practice a hermeneutics of good will and hospitality. Several articles in the volume refer in particular to the *Document on "Human Fraternity for World Peace and Living Together"* which was signed jointly by Pope Francis and the Grand Imam of Al-Azhar University, Ahamad al-Tayyib in February of 2019. This document strongly denounces all acts of violence committed in the name of religion, and declares "the adoption of a culture of dialogue as the path; mutual cooperation as the code of conduct; and reciprocal understanding as the method and standard." A dialogue that is often neglected is that between Protestant Churches and Islam. The migration of many Muslims into European countries in the course of the past five years has challenged these Churches to also develop more clear guidelines for dialogue.

Part II focuses on important models for Muslim-Christian friendship and engagement, and in particular on the figure of Christian de Chergé, the Trappist monk and prior whose life and death became a testament to love of the Muslim neighbour. His testimony was the inspiration behind the invitation of Muslims to the inter-monastic dialogue, which itself has opened the door to a deeper spiritual engagement between the two traditions in various parts of the world. De Chergé's own conception and experience of "a martyrdom of love" as a dedication of one's entire life to love of God and love of neighbour, may itself be regarded as an expression of theological hope.

Part III lifts up examples of constructive Muslim-Christian relations in different parts of the world. In Indonesia, both Muslims and Christians are charting new forms of national identity that include the religious other, partly in reaction to more extremist tendencies in both religions. In Germany, the establishment of chairs of Islamic theology at various universities allows for fruitful intellectual exchange and constructive conversation, building on a common intellectual and philosophical heritage. In Belgium, the Catholic Dialogue School model seeks to balance denominational identity with the skills necessary to live in a pluralist society, and thus may come to fulfil an exemplary and mediating role within the larger community. Turkey has been the place of important developments, both on the institutional and on the local level. Various popes have prayed together with Muslim leaders, and local organizations have sought to fill the gaps of ignorance and misunderstanding between the two communities. Nigeria has seen the rise of numerous Muslim and

Editorial

Christian interfaith organizations that work to counter the acts of violence committed by extremist groups like Boko Haram. And in the past five years, the Dominican Institute of Oriental Studies in Egypt has also witnessed a rise in interest on the part of Islamic institutions and individuals, eager to collaborate with and learn from scholarship in the humanities.

When focusing on the future of Muslim-Christian relations in Part IV, the focus on the Christian side is on the mutual recognition of both the universality and the particularity of the contending teachings of the two religions, on the recognition of moral failure on the part of both traditions, and on the mutual desire for academic collaboration and mutual religious probing. On the Muslim side, hope for the future is drawn from the various organizations, both Christian and Muslim, that stand up for the rights of both religions to practice their faith, and from our common belief in a good God that should be a "shield against the loss of hope."

In the Theological Forum, two millennial theologians reflect on the implications of the digital age for conducting public theology. They both point to the ambivalence of digital media for the dissemination of theology. While it facilitates the communication of seriously considered theological ideas to the broader public, it also opens up the proliferation of inflammatory and often uninformed theological positions that threaten the quality of theological discourse and the unity of the tradition.

Catherine Cornille, Daniel Franklin Pilario and Mile Babic

Part One: Official Statements and Documents

Nostra Aetate and Encounters of Friendship

WILHELMUS VALKENBERG

This article describes the development of official relationships in the international "dialogue of diplomacy" between Christian and Islamic religious leaders in the five decades after Nostra Aetate. The encounters of friendship that have developed over time are certainly signs of hope for better relationships even if political developments often seem to counteract these developments.

In its declaration on the relation of the Catholic Church to non-Christian religions *Nostra Aetate* (1965), the bishops of the Second Vatican Council famously describe the history of the relations between Christians and Muslims as including "not a few quarrels and hostilities."[1] Even though it is certainly true that such hostilities are more characteristic of the historical relationships between Christians and Muslims than dialogues and friendly encounters, some signs of hope can certainly be found, such as the encounter between Saint Francis of Assisi and Sultan al-Malik al-Kamil in Damietta (Egypt) in 1219, commemorated in quite a few places in 2019. The recent increase in encounters of friendship between Christians and Muslims certainly gives more reasons to be hopeful, even if it does not tell the entire story.[2] In this contribution I will concentrate on official statements and documents that mark this increase in encounters of friendship, mainly from the side of the Catholic Church, in the understanding that such statements and documents from other Christian and Islamic communities will be discussed elsewhere in this issue of *Concilium*. I start with the first signs of a new appreciation for Muslims as partners in dialogue in the documents of the Second Vatican Council and of Pope Paul VI. I add shorter discussions of the contributions made by the Pontifical Council for Interreligious Dialogue and its Commission for Religious Relations with Muslims, and by Popes John Paul II and Benedict XVI. I conclude with an impression of the new direction of the dialogue with Muslims that Pope Francis has suggested.

I "With Esteem": a new appreciation for Muslims

The third paragraph of the declaration *Nostra Aetate* begins with the words "[t]he Church also regards with esteem the Muslims."[3] The text continues by enumerating quite a few points of similarity:

> They adore the one God, who is living and subsisting in himself, merciful and all-powerful, the Creator of heaven and earth, who has spoken to humans; they strive to submit wholeheartedly even to His inscrutable decrees, just as Abraham, with whom the faith of Islam is gladly linked, submitted to God. Though they do not acknowledge Jesus as God, they revere him as a prophet. They also honour Mary, his virgin mother; at times, they even call on her with devotion. Moreover, they look forward to the day of judgment when God will reward all those raised up. For this reason, they value the moral life and worship God, especially through prayer, almsgiving and fasting.[4]

This enumeration of the faith, the practice and the spirituality of Muslims indicates a strong common ground. It is possible to distinguish at least five elements in this text that will be guiding future encounters in friendship between Catholics and Muslims. In the first place, Nostra Aetate is outspoken about the fact that Christians and Muslims adore the one God. This seems to be a radical statement that does not have many precedents in history, even though the text of the document contains a footnote referring to a letter of Pope Gregory VII to al-Nasir, king of Mauritania, written in 1076 as if to underscore continuity of doctrine.[5] In recent history, this continuity is most clearly stated in the dogmatic constitution *Lumen Gentium* where the Church says that Muslims "along with us adore the one and merciful God." The second element is the somewhat convoluted reference to Abraham: "just as Abraham, with whom the faith of Islam is gladly linked, submitted to God." The Council acknowledges the fact that Islam considers Abraham a model of one "who submits to God" (*muslim* in Arabic), as it did already in the text of *Lumen Gentium* 16: "the Muslims, who, professing to hold the faith of Abraham, along with us adore the one and merciful God".⁶ In the footsteps of the French Islamicist Louis Massignon (1883-1962), the Second Vatican Council recognizes that Muslims claim to share the faith of Abraham, even though there is some hesitancy to make this a common characteristic of so-called "Abrahamic religions".⁷ The third element of esteem for Muslims consists of a difference and a possible way forward: Muslims do not acknowledge Jesus as God, yet they revere him as prophet. Whereas the denial of the divinity of Christ has been taken by some Christians as a reason to deny the possibility of any theological dialogue with Islam, other Christian and Muslim theologians have successfully explored the possibilities of this theological dialogue concerning Jesus.⁸ In comparison, the fourth element mentioned in *Nostra Aetate* strikes a very positive note: Muslims honour Mary as virgin mother of Jesus and sometimes call on her with devotion. This devotional aspect creates space for new dimensions in Christian – Muslim relationships.⁹ The fifth element connects the expectation of the Day of Judgment, which is a central element in the Qur'an, with the notion of human responsibility and thus with moral and practical elements of the Islamic faith. In fact, it is this ethical and practical dimension of dialogue that is singled out for consideration at the end of *Nostra Aetate* 3: "But now this Sacred Synod pleads with all to forget the past, to make sincere efforts for mutual understanding, and so to work together for the preservation and fostering of social justice, moral welfare, and peace and freedom for all humankind."¹⁰ These words are significant because they determine the type of dialogue that is favoured by the Vatican authorities in their contacts with Muslims: a dialogue that focuses on ethical values and possibilities for practical collaboration, and not a specifically theological dialogue as is the case in the relationship with Jews.¹¹

II The Catholic Church and Dialogue after *Nostra Aetate*

The history of the Second Vatican Council started with its announcement by Pope John XXIII in January 1959 and it ended under the pontificate of Pope Paul VI in December 1965. The influences of both popes are clearly visible in *Nostra Aetate*, but also in the permanent *dicasteria* or forms of administration that were founded to guarantee a lasting involvement of the Roman Catholic Church in dialogue worldwide. After the French historian Jules Isaac met with Pope John XXIII in 1960 to remind him of the fateful history of the Church's teaching of contempt, the pope wanted to include a statement about the Jews in the documents of the council and asked the newly instituted Secretariat for Promoting Christian Unity to prepare such a document. The history of the document *Nostra Aetate* thus started with a document about the relationship with the Jews, and this relationship has remained under the auspices of the Secretariat – later Pontifical Council – for Promoting Christian Unity ever since. However, Pope Paul VI wanted to include dialogue with Muslims as he announced on his trip to the Holy Land in January 1964, and in his encyclical *Ecclesiam Suam*.[12] Therefore, the secretariat added specialists on Islam and South- and East-Asian religions to the writers of Nostra Aetate in October 1964. Most of them were missionaries who were advisors to the bishops of the areas where they worked in Asia or the Middle East.[13] In the activities of the Secretariat for Non-Christians, established by Pope Paul VI in 1964 and renamed Pontifical Council for Interreligious Dialogue by Pope John Paul II in 1988, the relations between dialogue and mission remained a focal point, as appears from the titles of the two most important documents that it published: "Reflections and Orientations on Dialogue and Mission" (1984), and "Dialogue and Proclamation" (1991).[14] However important these documents may be, the encounters and forms of collaboration with partner organizations are probably the most important developments facilitated by the Pontifical Council for Interreligious Dialogue in the fifty years since *Nostra Aetate*, and this holds certainly true for the dialogue with Muslims.[15] One text deserves particular attention because it has been written specifically with a view on the dialogue between Christians and Muslims: "Guidelines for Dialogue between Christians and Muslims," originally published in 1970 and rewritten by Fr. Maurice Borrmans M. Afr. (1925-2017) in collaboration with Fr. Arij Roest Crollius.[16] The document begins with a description of the partners in dialogue with an emphasis on the diversity in the world of Islam. The second chapter sketches the different places and paths of dialogue, distinguishing between the basic 'dialogue of living together' and the more specific levels and forms of dialogues between believers. The central chapter commends a specific method of approaching Islam, in which Christians start to look at the practices of Muslims, and then proceed to discern the values and ideas behind these practices. After this follows a practical chapter that investigates ways to overcome mutual prejudices: not only Christian forms of Islamophobia, but also Muslim prejudices against Christianity. The chapter ends with a sobering account of remaining obstacles. In the line of chapter five suggests a number of areas where Christians and Muslims can cooperate at the practical level: the care for God's creation, service to humankind, and promoting human dignity. Chapter six, finally, enumerates potential areas of religious cooperation that may lead to a development of spirituality that is open to mutual enrichment. The document gives suggestions to further dialogue between Catholic Christians and Muslims at the practical and the spiritual levels, not so much at the theological level. This is the basic approach that Pope John Paul II would take as well.

III Popes John Paul II and Benedict XVI

It is possible to see a strong continuity between the endeavours by Pope John Paul II (1978-2005) and Pope Benedict XVI (2005-2013) since Joseph Cardinal Ratzinger served as prefect of the Congregation for the Doctrine of the Faith from 1981 until he became pope, and was therefore closely connected to all interfaith initiatives in which Pope John Paul II engaged. He did not always agree with John Paul's initiatives such as the organization of a day of prayer for world peace in Assisi in 1986. This was a grand-scale ecumenical and interreligious event in which representatives of different religions prayed in different places before convening with the Pope at a closing ceremony.[17] Even though the event was organized as a way to pray in one another's presence, and not as a "praying together," quite a few conservative Catholics criticized it as smacking of syncretism and relativism.[18] Cardinal Ratzinger, who was among these critics, would nevertheless participate in later instalments of the World Day of Prayer for Peace, for instance at its 25th anniversary in 2011. Though one may find substantial differences in the theological opinions of both popes about interfaith relationships, yet these differences seem to vanish with a view to the large symbolic impact of these encounters. For instance, Pope Benedict gave a very controversial speech about the harmony of faith and reason when he visited his old colleagues at the University of Regensburg in September 2006, but he seemed to pray alongside the Imam in the Blue Mosque when he visited Istanbul a month later.[19] At the same time, a spontaneous interaction with people of other faiths seemed to come more naturally to the pastorally oriented Polish bishop who was influenced by deep friendships with Jews from the beginning of his ecclesial career than to the theologian from Bavaria who tended to shy away from interactions with revolutionary students in Tübingen and focus more on preserving the identity of the Christian tradition. It needs to be said that the perception of the differences between the two popes is strongly influenced by the change in receptivity toward religious others in Europe from the end of the 1990s onwards. Certainly after Sept. 11, 2001, the relationship with Muslims began to gain importance in both the Pontifical Council for Interreligious Dialogue and the Interreligious Office of the World Council of Churches, while at the same time conservative Christian voices that denounced theological common ground with Islam gained importance.[20] Anja Middelbeck-Varwick summarizes the change nicely by saying: when Pope John Paul II, addressing Muslim youth in Casablanca (1985), said that "we believe in the same God, the one God, the living God," people agreed with him and praised him. Yet when Pope Francis repeats the same words in recent statements, this is seen as a "daring" or "courageous" statement that is not accepted by a good number of Christians in Europe.[21] The era of Pope Francis gives us signs of hope in two respects: his new approach to Christian – Muslim dialogue, and a shift of the centre of this dialogue from the West to the Middle East.

IV Dialogue and Human Fraternity: Pope Francis

When Pope Francis announced his visit to Palestine and the Holy Land in 2014, he followed in the footsteps of his predecessors. The significant difference, however, was that he included a Jewish and a Muslim friend in the papal delegation. His friendship with Rabbi Abraham Skorka is well-known and dates from before the moment that Jorge Bergoglio became archbishop of Buenos Aires in 1998.[22] The second significant gesture that Pope Francis made was to invite the presidents of Israel and Palestine, Shimon Peres and Mahmoud Abbas, to a 'Prayer Summit' with him and Patriarch Bartholomew in the Vatican gardens a month later. This gesture is characteristic for Pope Francis who has emphasized the necessity of prayer on many occasions in his interreligious encounters.[23] Another characteristic of Pope Francis' approach to interreligious encounters is the stress on friendship and human fraternity.[24] Recently, this characteristic has become eminently visible in the document that Pope Francis co-signed in Abu Dhabi on February 4, 2019 with Ahmad el-Tayyeb, the Grand Imam of Al-Azhar, "On Human Fraternity for World Peace and Living Together."[25] Even though it is too early to tell if this document will gain a better reception than most other interreligious documents, the two parties involved want to take it seriously by publishing follow-up documents and appointing a committee – now including Jewish rabbis as well – that coordinates further actions.[26] Another sign of hope in Christian – Muslim relations is that the centre of gravity seems to shift from Europe towards the Middle East since the Vatican – and on certain occasions the World Council of Churches as well – are now more frequently involved in initiatives that find their origins in countries such as Jordan, Morocco, Saudi Arabia, Iran, and the United Arab Emirates.[27] Even though it is clear that these initiatives often serve political goals, it is significant that a thick web of interreligious encounters between Christians and Muslims is beginning to develop that will not easily be undone by future backlashes. The fact that this web develops in the area where Christians are now dwindling minorities gives certainly reason for hope.

Notes

1. Translation by Thomas F. Stransky, CSP (1930-2019), one of the original contributors to Nostra Aetate in Pim Valkenberg/Anthony Cirelli (eds), *Nostra Aetate: Celebrating 50 Years of the Catholic Church's Dialogue with Jews and Muslims*, Washington D.C.: The Catholic University of America Press, 2016, xxi.
2. See also Douglas Pratt, "Initiative and Response: The Future of Muslim – Christian Dialogue", in Paul Hedges (ed.), *Contemporary Muslim – Christian Encounters: Developments, Diversity and Dialogues*, London: Bloomsbury, 2015, 117-133.
3. Nostra Aetate 3, tr. Stransky. See also Anja Middelbeck-Varwick, *Cum Aestimatione: Konturen einer christlichen Islamtheologie*, Münster: Aschendorff, 2017
4. *Nostra Aetate* 3, translation Stransky, xx-xxi.
5. See Gavin D'Costa, *Vatican II: Catholic Doctrines on Jews & Muslims*, Oxford: Oxford University Press, 2014, 205-208.
6. Translation according to Vatican website, www.vatican.va. See also D'Costa, *Vatican II*, 169-75.
7. See also Pim Valkenberg, "Does the Concept of 'Abrahamic Religions' have a Future?"

Wilhelmus Valkenberg

Concilium 2005/5, 103-111

8. See, among others, Oddbjorn Leirvik, *Images of Jesus Christ in Islam*, London, 2010; Mona Siddiqui, *Christians, Muslims & Jesus*, New Haven, 2013; Zeki Saritoprak, *Islam's Jesus*, Gainesville, 2014; Klaus von Stosch/Mouhanad Khorchide, *Streit um Jesus: muslimische und christliche Annäherungen*, Paderborn, 2016; Mustafa Akyol, *The Islamic Jesus*, New York, 2017.

9. See Mary Thurlkill, *Chosen Among Women: Mary and Fatima in Medieval Christianity and Shi'ite Islam*, Notre Dame IN, 2007; Rita George-Tvrtlović, *Christians, Muslims, and Mary: A History*, New York, 2018.

10. *Nostra Aetate*, 3, transl. Stransky, xxi.

11. *Nostra Aetate* 4 mentions biblical and theological studies as an important source for mutual understanding and esteem in relationship with Jews. This element is absent in *Nostra Aetate* 3. See Pim Valkenberg, 'The Academic Reception of Nostra Aetate', in: *Nostra Aetate: Celebrating 50 Years of the Catholic Church's Dialogue with Jews and Muslims*, 253-263.

12. Pope Paul VI, "Message to the World", Bethlehem, January 6, 1964. Translation in: *Pontifical Council for Interreligious Dialogue*, In Francesco Gioia (ed.) *Interreligious Dialogue: The Official Teaching of the Catholic Church from the Second Vatican Council to John Paul II* (1963-2005), Boston: Pauline Books and Media, 2006, 159.

13. Pim Valkenberg, "Nostra Aetate: Historical Contingency and Theological Significance", in: *Nostra Aetate: Celebrating 50 Years of the Catholic Church's Dialogue with Jews and Muslims*, 6-26 (information based on the Council diaries of J. Willebrands and Y. Congar.)

14. English translations in *Interreligious Dialogue: The Official Teaching of the Catholic Church from the Second Vatican Council to John Paul II* (1963-2005), 1116-1129 and 1156-1189.

15. A short survey by Cardinal Tauran, President of the Pontifical Council for Interreligious Dialogue between 2007 and his death in 2018, in: *Nostra Aetate: Celebrating 50 Years of the Catholic Church's Dialogue with Jews and Muslims*, 93-99. Longer surveys in ecumenical perspective: Clare Amos, "Vatican and World Council of Churches Initiatives: Weaving Interreligious Threads on Ecumenical Looms", in Paul Hedges (ed.), *Contemporary Muslim – Christian Encounters, 185-200*; Risto Jukko, Douglas Pratt and Michael Ipgrave, "The Churches and Christian – Muslim Relations", in David Thomas (ed.), *Routledge Handbook on Christian – Muslim Relations*, London and New York: Routledge, 2018, 247-256.

16. An English translation was published as *Guidelines for Dialogue between Christians and Muslims*, Mahwah N.J. / New York: Paulist Press, 1990.

17. The picture of this closing ceremony has been used many times, for instance on the cover of the book *John Paul II and Interreligious Dialogue*, Byron Sherwin/Harold Kasimow (eds.) Maryknoll NY: Orbis, 1999. Representatives of Christian traditions stand to the right of the pope, and representatives of South- and East-Indian religions to his left. By contrast, Jews and Muslims are conspicuously absent in this picture.

18. For the contents of the World Day of Prayer for Peace, see *Bulletin Secretariatus pro non Christianis* 22 (1987), 11-60. For a theological reflection, see Gerda Riedl, *Modell Assisi: christliches Gebet und interreligiöser Dialog in heilsgeschichtlichem Kontext*, Berlin 1998.

19. This "Regensburg address" belongs to the pre-history of the "Common Word document" that will be discussed in the next article of this volume.

20. See specifics in Amos, "Vatican and World Council of Churches Initiatives", 194-198.

21. See Middelbeck-Varwick, *Cum Aestimatione*, 218. Translation of the words of Pope John Paul II in Casablanca according to *Interreligious Dialogue: The Official Teaching of the Catholic Church from the Second Vatican Council to John Paul II (1963-2005)*, 337. See also Pim Valkenberg, "*A Common Word* or a Word of Justice? Two Qur'anic Approaches to Christian-Muslim Dialogue', in Yazid Said/Lejla Demiri (eds.) *The Future of Interfaith Dialogue. Muslim – Christian Encounters through A Common Word*, Cambridge, Cambridge University Press, 2018, 192-203.

22. See Abraham Skorka, "Foreword: Who is Jorge Bergoglio?" in Harold Kasimov/Alan Race (eds.) *Pope Francis and Interreligious Dialogue: Religious Thinkers Engage with Recent Papal Initiatives*, Cham: Springer, 2018, vii-xii.

23. In his first address on the balcony after being appointed, Pope Francis asked the people to pray for him. For references to prayer in interreligious encounters, see *Pope Francis and Interreligious Dialogue*, 26, 42, 52, 57, 69 and 72.

24. See James L. Fredericks, "Nostra Aetate and Pope Francis: Reflections on the Next Fifty Years of Catholic Dialogue with Buddhists," in Valkenberg/Cirelli (eds.) *Nostra Aetate: Celebrating 50 Years of the Catholic Church's Dialogue with Jews and Muslims*, 43-57.

25. The document is published on the website of the Pontifical Council for Interreligious Dialogue: https://www.pcinterreligious.org/document-human-fraternity-translations

26. See https://www.pcinterreligious.org/documents-on-human-fraternity

27. From the point of view of the Catholic Church, the involvement of Msgr. Miguel Ángel Cardinal Ayuso Guixot (Spain) and Msgr. Khaled Akashed (Jordan), president and secretary of the PCID's Committee for Religious Relations with Muslims is crucial.

A Common Word between Us and You – a Carrier of Hope

VEBJØRN L. HORSFJORD

The document A Common Word Between Us and You *was published by a broad range of Muslim leaders and scholars in October 2007. Focussing on the twin commandment to love God and neighbour, it invited Christian leaders to engage in dialogue. Many Church leaders eagerly embraced the invitation, and in the subsequent years, the Muslim initiative bore fruits in the form of numerous Muslim-Christian conferences and cooperative projects across the world involving a broad range of Christians from Orthodox to Evangelicals. It has inspired interreligious cooperation beyond the Muslim-Christian axis and can continue to do so in the years to come.*

> The [UN] General Assembly…proclaims the first week of February every year the World Interfaith Harmony Week between all religions, faiths and beliefs; [and] encourages all States to support, on a voluntary basis, the spread of the message of interfaith harmony and goodwill in the world's churches, mosques, synagogues, temples, and other places of worship during that week, based on love of God and love of one's neighbour or on love of the good and love of one's neighbour, each according to their own religious traditions or convictions…[1]

October 2020 will mark the 10th anniversary of the unanimous UNGA resolution that established the World Interfaith Harmony Week. With its semi-theological language on God and the good, clearly inspired by Biblical language on love for God and neighbour, the resolution is unusual, but it is also reflective of a widely shared desire to counter narratives of increasing interreligious tensions. The resolution was proposed by the Kingdom of Jordan. Via Jordan and its Royal Aal al-Bayt Institute for Islamic Thought (RABIIT) in Amman, there runs an indirect, but clear line from Pope Benedict XVI's controversial Regensburg lecture in September 2006 to the World Interfaith Harmony Week. In 2009, the pope used language similar to that found in the UN resolution when he spoke to Muslim leaders at the Al-Aqsa mosque in Jerusalem: 'Undivided love for the One God and charity towards one's neighbour thus become the fulcrum around which all else turns.' The idea that the twin love commandment should be the basis for interreligious understanding originated in the document *A Common Word Between Us and You* (ACW) from October 2007, a text of about 15 pages sent by 138 prominent Muslim leaders and scholars as an open letter to the pope and other Christian leaders.

A Common Word became one of the most dynamic initiatives for dialogue among Christians and Muslims in the first decade of this century, and it continues to produce fruit. In what follows, I will present the content and background of the document. Then I will share some critical comments before I move on to distil four aspects of ACW and the subsequent dialogue process that I suggest carry hope for the future: The use of modern technology to promote interreligious understanding; the application of a 'hermeneutics of good will' in interreligious encounters; the potential of ACW to function as an Islamic Nostra Aetate; and the entire dialogue process' character of performance and modelling for local dialogue initiatives.

I Content and background

The core argument in *A Common Word* is spelt out in its first paragraphs: "The Unity of God, the necessity of love for Him, and the necessity of love of the neighbour is thus the common ground between Islam and Christianity." The authors contend that this common ground on which Christians and Muslims should meet, can be found in the holy scriptures of both traditions. The text, which has the flavour of a theological treatise, contains extensive quotes from the Qur'an (30 per cent of the entire text) and the Bible (10 per cent) as well as a number of Hadiths. Its three parts first discuss love of God, then love of neighbour, and lastly argue that Christians and Muslims should enter into dialogue and cooperation based on the common ground identified in the first two parts.

The central contention that faith in one god and the twin love commandments is shared by Muslims and Christians (as well as Jews) is not new.[2] However, it is novel that a text that carries the authority of a wide collection of Islamic scholars consistently uses concepts that have their origin in the Bible as a prism to understand the Qur'an. Specific wording mandating love for God and love for neighbour, and the notion that these constitute 'commandments', are not found in the Qur'an or elsewhere in Islamic tradition. In ACW a number of central quotes from the Qur'an and Hadith are interpreted in light of these Biblical concepts and shown – in the authors' opinion – to be equivalent to these Biblical concepts. The substantive and theological significance of this equivalence is reinforced with a reference to the Islamic conviction that the central characters of Jewish and Christian tradition, including Moses and Jesus, were prophets sent by God, and that Muhammad as the final messenger in principle brought 'nothing new'. This is laid out in the slightly intricate, but very important final paragraph of the part of the text that deals with love for God:

> [W]e can now perhaps understand the words [by Muhammad] 'The best that I have said – myself, and the prophets that came before me' as equating the blessed formula 'There is no god but God, He Alone, He hath no associate, His is the sovereignty and His is the praise and He hath power over all things' precisely with the 'First and Greatest Commandment' to love God with all one's heart and soul, as found in various places in the Bible.

The authors find the Islamic tradition's equivalent of the commandment to love neighbour in the Hadith '[N]one of you has faith until you love for your neighbour what you love for yourself'. Although this does not literally command love for neighbour, it is a rare example in Islamic scriptures of relating the words 'love' and 'neighbour' to each other.

When *A Common Word* was published, it contained a list of 138 signatories. The signatures are integral to its message. Among the Islamic scholars and leaders were some of the world's most prominent representatives of both Sunni and Shia Islam, and they represent 40 different countries. The list conveys the message that *A Common Word* is more than a theological treatise: In it we hear the voice of diverse and nevertheless unified representatives of Islam.

The signatories were listed alphabetically (according to the English spelling of their names), and none were identified as the leading authors. However, from the beginning, it was assumed that the document to a large extent had been written by Prince Ghazi bin Muhammad of Jordan, King Abdullah II's cousin and the director of the Aal Al-Bayt Institute. Later Ghazi let it be known that he was not only a leading author, but ACW's sole author.[3]

One year prior to *A Common Word*, Prince Ghazi joined by 37 other Islamic leaders, had published another open letter addressed to Pope Benedict. This first open letter was a direct reaction to the pope's lecture at the University in Regensburg on 12 September 2006 in which he was heard to associate Islam with violence. The letter invited the pope to continue dialogue on topics of Islamic scriptural interpretation on which he, according to Ghazi, was mistaken. As a direct follow up, work on ACW began.

Like the first open letter, *A Common Word* is addressed first and foremost to the pope, and then to a series of 26 other senior church leaders. The list of addressees mirrors the list of signatories and suggests that ACW initiates an exchange between the most senior representatives of Christians and Muslims in the world.

II The ACW dialogue process

Precisely what Prince Ghazi and his collaborators expected would be the outcome of *A Common Word*, is not fully clear, but there is no doubt that they envisioned some form of response from senior church leaders.[4] In fact, some such responses were integral to the carefully managed publication of the document when the (Anglican) bishop of London and the Archbishop of Canterbury immediately offered their short but appreciative comments. The pope was, however, slow in responding. In the longer run, the Vatican caught up and made Ghazi and *A Common Word* one of their priorities in Catholic – Muslim dialogue. The Catholic-Muslim forum was established and met first in Rome in November 2008 to discuss precisely 'Love for God, Love for Neighbour.' They met again in 2011, 2014 and 2017.

The Archbishop of Canterbury, Rowan Williams, followed up his first welcoming comments with intra-Christian (ecumenical) consultations as well as a high profile Christian-Muslim conference in Cambridge. He also produced a substantive theological text, considerably longer than *A Common Word* itself, in which he responded to a number of the topics present in the Muslim leaders' letter.[5]

In the US, Christian theologians at Yale University wrote an appreciative response and collected signatures from senior US based Christian leaders, notably a wide range of Evangelical leaders. Their text, also theological in nature, was presented to the public as a full page advertisement in the New York Times a month after ACW's publication, in November 2007. Later followed a high profile conference of senior Christian and Muslim leaders at Yale as well as one at Georgetown University in Washington DC.

The World Council of Churches – like the Vatican – made Ghazi and RABIIT a key partner in dialogue with the Muslim world. Their cooperation emphasised the peacebuilding potential of interreligious understanding. The partnership especially focussed on Nigeria with various concrete initiatives to improve Christian-Muslim relations in this country divided between Christians and Muslims and haunted by violent clashes and terrorism. Ghazi went on a high profile mission to the country jointly with the WCC Secretary General, Olav Fykse Tveit.

The *A Common Word* website documents a vast number of responses to ACW also from various other senior Christian leaders. Some of them are very substantive such as the one sent by Alexy II, the Patriarch of Moscow and leader of the world's biggest Orthodox church.

III Critical comments

A Common Word met with almost overwhelming positive responses from church leaders and many others. However, it is not without its faults and limitations. Critical comments have been forthcoming, not only from those whose scepticism towards Islam or interreligious dialogue is such that almost any dialogue initiative would trigger negative comments, but also from quarters who sympathise with interreligious dialogue generally. Some, such as Bishop Michael Nazir-Ali, the Church of England bishop of Rochester with long experience from interreligious dialogue, have pointed out that ACW seems to insist on a specific Islamic understanding of God's oneness (*tawheed*) as basis for mutual Christian-Muslim understanding. They ask whether the authors expect Christians to give up central parts of their Trinitarian faith. Along the same line, some have asked whether ACW's reading of Biblical texts imposes an Islamic understanding of Jesus role (as a prophet rather than Son of God and saviour) on the Biblical material. Such critics also ask whether the choice of Qur'anic texts is so eclectic that ACW is unsound on Islamic theology's own terms.[6]

A different, but substantial, criticism regards gender. ACW is completely oblivious to the gender dimension of religion and interreligious dialogue. All the addressees and almost all the signatories are men. This point is also closely connected to ACW's focus on religious leadership. The underlying assumption seems to be that the most senior religious leaders can represent all co-religionists, and that their normative understandings of their traditions are accepted unquestioningly by those for whom they are leaders. This absolutely disregards insights into the difference between normative traditions and 'lived religion', the fact that there is often an enormous gap between religion as taught by religious authorities and religion as lived by ordinary people.

Throughout the text, the argument rests on the assumption that 'Muslims' and 'Christians' are meaningful categories. Such essensialisation of grand categories may not only give rise to flawed analyses of the world, but may in fact contribute to reinforcing differences and increasing the importance of religious identification, which is the exact opposite of the stated intention.[7]

The follow up of *A Common Word* in the form of international conferences, formal dialogues and cooperation has been unprecedented. Although better than most other similar initiatives, even this process suffers from an absence of long-term commitment from many of the participants. Formal responses and conference statements in the wake of ACW almost all point to further follow up – topics that should be explored in greater depth, cooperative projects that should be undertaken. Too often, these have not materialized. Unfulfilled expectations are a problem not only because good projects are not implemented, but because creating a series of unfulfilled promises may undermine faith in interreligious dialogue and create 'dialogue fatigue'.

Some of the criticism of ACW is substantial and should be considered very carefully. I have written in more depth about it elsewhere.[8] However, both much of the criticism and the signs of hope derived from ACW arise from the same feature of the text: It is open, sometimes ambiguous and thus contains a surplus of meaning that invites interpreters to do their own interpretative work on it. In the remainder of this article, I will point out some of the signs of hope that can be found in ACW's many layers.

IV Theology and technology

A Common Word contains little explicit analysis of contemporary society, and there is no mention of technology. In one sense, ACW is almost timeless. However, it is hard to imagine a similar initiative much earlier in history. The launch and dissemination were key factors in its success. A recognised PR company, Bell Pottinger, played a central role in this.[9] The document was launched simultaneously in Europe and the US. It appeared to the public together with welcoming statements from a senior politician, Tony Blair, as well as senior church leaders and respected academics. Thus it was immediately in the global (or at least Western) news cycle and widely reported. News reporting played together with the ACW website so that the audience could not only read about the document, but immediately access it themselves. Soon, the website was the centre of what became the ACW process through which several hundred responses were collected. It documented that a great diversity of religious leaders and scholars were engaging with the document and thus inspired others to do the same.

One of the most important features of the many international conferences in the wake of ACW was their reporting through the media. As I will suggest below, dialogue among senior religious leaders is performance, and the performances reached their audience through modern media. Photos and videos of such conferences literally make visible friendly relations across religious dividing lines. In many cases, they became available on the ACW website.

ACW was launched before smart phones with their 'social media' apps became ubiquitous, but used the most advanced information technology at the time to create impact. It is hard to see how something similar could have been achieved 20 or even only ten years earlier, when mail was analogue and films only available on linear TV. ACW was a fairly successful attempt at creating a counter discourse to that of a clash of civilisations and increasing interreligious tensions. To achieve its effect, it used exactly the same media that amplify discord. It demonstrates the potential of modern communication technology to improve intercultural communication and foster understanding across traditional dividing lines.

V An Islamic Nostra Aetate?

What is the central suggestion in *A Common Word*? Several slightly different interpretations are possible: It can be read as an invitation to enter into interreligious dialogue to explore together God's oneness, and love for God and neighbour. Or it can be seen as an invitation to Christians to enter into dialogue and cooperation on the basis that agreement on these topics already exists. Both readings have merit, but each is also difficult to reconcile with specific details of the text. Yet another reading would be to see it as reciprocating *Nostra Aetate*.

For five decades *Nostra Aetate* has been the basis on which the Catholic Church has met Muslims and people of other faiths, making transparent to all parties how the church theologically views its involvement in dialogue. A similar Islamic outline of a theology of religions has never been produced. With its broad support among Muslim leaders and scholars, ACW could fill this role.

About Muslims *Nostra Aetate* says in article 3: "The Church regards with esteem also the Moslems. They adore the one God, living and subsisting in Himself. ...Though they do not acknowledge Jesus as God, they revere Him as a prophet. They also honour Mary, His virgin Mother." *Nostra Aetate* does not invite Muslims to agree with its theology, which they clearly could not do since it expresses an unmistakeably Christian understanding of God. Its message is that this is how far Catholics in good conscience can go in recognising value in Islamic teaching.

If we read *A Common Word* as a mirror image of this, Christians do not need to accept the document's interpretation of the Bible or its understanding of God's oneness. Rather, they can read the document as saying: This is how far Islamic scholars in good conscience can reach out to Christians and recognise their striving. As *Nostra Aetate* recognises that Muslims have come far in their understanding of Jesus and Mary, although not captured the full (Catholic) truth, so ACW could suggest that Christians have come far in their understanding of what love for God and

God's oneness imply, although they have not captured the full (Islamic) truth. Thus ACW invites dialogue and cooperation, but not necessarily on its own content nor assuming agreement on these matters. Rather, it signals openness and that the starting assumption is the good intention of the other.

VI A Hermeneutics of Good Will

Mutual suspicion has often been a feature of Christian – Muslim relations. A hermeneutics of suspicion is a valuable reading strategy in many contexts. By not taking a text (or its author) on face value, it can damask power asymmetries and provide a basis for deeper analysis of interpersonal and societal relations. However, in interreligious relations (as in many other relationships), it can be detrimental to have as a starting assumption that people and texts don't mean what they appear to say.[10]

A Common Word's reading of the Bible may be criticised for picking and choosing those elements in the Bible that best correspond to Islamic theology. However, this may also be its strength. The authors make an extra effort to read the Christian text in a positive light. Not only do they take it on face value, but they use a bit of force, exert a strong will, to make it acceptable on Islamic terms. Similar reading strategies can be observed repeatedly in the subsequent exchange of responding texts. From ACW's overflow of potential meaning, Christian respondents focus on that which best corresponds to their interests and ideals for interreligious dialogue. Parts of ACW which are difficult from a Christian point of view – for example the repeated emphasis on God's oneness that historically has had the function of condemning Trinitarian teaching – is left aside, and that which is seen to help the dialogue forward, is amplified. Many Christian respondents pay more attention to the good intention they discern from behind the text, and the 'tone' they find in the text, than its specific arguments. This is a choice, a reading strategy, and does not simply come naturally. In a document defending Evangelicals who signed the Yale response that expressed strong appreciation of ACW, the European Evangelical Alliance explicitly endorses such a hermeneutics of good will: '[T]hey *chose* to believe the best about the Muslim people who signed "*A Common Word*": *interpreting* it as a brave and generous step' [emphases added].[11]

VII Counter narrative and performance

Together those behind ACW and the Christian leaders who involved themselves in the subsequent conferences and exchange of documents, created a counter narrative to that of a clash of civilisations or religions. However, the dialogue process goes beyond discourse and narrative. I will suggest that it can be understood in terms of gestures and performance, and that it concretely models peaceful interreligious interaction for local Muslim and Christian communities.

Something similar to ACW would probably have appeared even without Pope Benedict's Regensburg lecture, but there is little doubt that that incident triggered the process. While some Islamists reacted violently to the pope's lecture and many Muslim leaders condemned it in strong words, Ghazi chose a different path. His first open letter was an invitation to dialogue. Instead of hitting back at what many saw as an insult, his text can be seen as turning the other cheek. Ghazi has made no secret of his disappointment at the Vatican's lack of response to his gesture, but rather than letting disappointment fuel an aggressive move, he produced ACW, again turning the other cheek.[12]

The authors of the Yale response in their turn explicitly interpreted ACW as 'a Muslim hand of conviviality and cooperation'. Their response was to 'extend our Christian hand in return'. Together, Christian and Muslim leaders thus created discursive images of Muslims and Christians meeting in friendship. These were followed up by actual, physical meetings which projected the same message.

A limitation, however, of these gestures and meetings is the relationship between those who meet (specific religious leaders) and the much broader groups they claim to speak for ('Muslims' and 'Christians'). Religious leaders do not represent their co-religionists in any formal or binding way. Political leaders, for example, can make legally binding commitments on behalf of the countries they represent. Religious leaders, however, lead by other mechanisms. Their promises and admissions on behalf of 'Christians' and 'Muslims' are not binding and cannot be taken literally. It is better to understand them as a form of performance. The religious leaders act out cordial relationships and thus model for their co-religionists potentially new ways of interacting with those of other faiths. When other Christians and Muslims in local communities across the globe emulate the senior leaders who created the ACW process, *A Common Word* achieves its goal even when love for God and neighbour is not the focus of interreligious interaction.

VIII A carrier of hope

The first decades of the 21st century has seen Muslim-Christian relations at the centre of international politics. Many long for relationships across religious boundaries that are suited to a time of rapid technological advances, mass migration and climate change. The UN resolution on interfaith harmony in October 2010 gave voice to such longing also from those who do not ordinarily trade in interreligious dialogue. The *A Common Word* initiative, despite its faults and limitations, carries hope for the future. The world needs religions leaders who can be models for cordial relationships in local communities. We need examples of open hermeneutics, wilfully looking for points of agreement rather than discord. We need statements of theologies of religions that build on such openness in interpreting the other. And we need examples of how new technologies can be put to the service of the forces of good. Perhaps the world even needs to be nudged towards pondering such an allusive but often misused concept as love.

Notes

1. United Nations General Assembly, Resolution adopted by the General Assembly: World Interfaith Harmony Week (A/RES/65/5) [Online], New York: United Nations (2010). Available from: <https://undocs.org/en/A/RES/65/5> [accessed 24 November 2019]
2. Tom Heneghan, 'At Dome of Rock, Benedict uses Muslims' argument to Muslims', Reuters [Online], (2009) Available from: <http://blogs.reuters.com/faithworld/2009/05/12/at-dome-of-rock-benedict-uses-muslims-argument-to-muslims/> [accessed 22 November 2019]
3. Oddbjørn Leirvik, "'Aw qāla: 'Li-jārihi': some observations on brotherhood and neighborly love in Islamic tradition," In Islam and Christian-Muslim Relations, 21, (2010), 357–372.
4. Strikingly absent from most discussions on ACW are references to Feisal Abdul Rauf who three years prior to ACW advanced a similar argument in a very similar form in his book *What is right with Islam: a new vision for Muslims and the West*, San Francisco: Harper, 2004. Rauf is among the signatories to ACW, but nowhere credited as a contributor to its key content.
5. All the Christian responses referred to in this article are available at www.acommonword.com

6. Lutz Richter-Bernburg, *A common word between us and you: observations on the (mis)uses of koranic exegesis in interreligious dialogue* [Online], Tübingen: University of Tübingen (2008). Available from: <http://tobias-lib.uni-tuebingen.de/volltexte/2009/3940/pdf/Lutz_Richter_Bernburg.pdf> [accessed 22 November 2019]
7. Pamela Klassen and Courtney Bender, 'Introduction: habits of pluralims'. In Bender/Klassen (eds.), *After pluralism: reimagining religious engagement*, New York: Columbia University Press, 2010, 10.
8. For a further discussion of 'dialogue fatigue' see V. L. Horsfjord, 'The Marrakesh Declaration on Rights of Religious Minorities: Opportunity or Dead End?', *Nordic Journal of Human Rights*, 36:2 (2018), 151-166.
9. Sarah L. Markiewicz, The genesis and fruits of the open letter 'A Common Word between Us and You' (2007), [Dr. theol thesis], Berlin: Humboldt-Universität zu Berlin, 2014, 189.
10. Bernd Wannenwetsch, *Political worship: ethics for Christian citizens,* Oxford: Oxford University Press, 2004, 289.
11. European Evangelical Alliance, Beyond polite dialogue? [Online] (2008), available from: <https://www.worldea.org/news/1802/European-Evangelical-Alliance-Beyond-Polite-DialougeThoughts-and-responses-to-A-Common-Word> [accessed 24 November 2019]
12. Ghazi bin Muhammad, 'On "A Common Word between Us and You"', in Miroslav Volf/Ghazi bin Muhammad/Melissa Yarrington (eds.), *A Common Word: Muslims and Christians on loving God and neighbour*, Grand Rapids: William B. Eerdmans Publishing Company, 2010, 8.

Migration as a Kairos Moment for Protestant-Muslim Dialogue

JOSHUA RALSTON

This essay examines how the migration crisis of 2015 presented churches in Europe with a 'kairos' moment that demanded fresh theological reflection on Islam and social action alongside Muslims. By exploring how the initial comments and public pronouncements by churches in 2015 focused very little on Islam and Muslims, I argue that churches failed to challenge political appeals that presented Christendom as locked in a recurring battle with Islam. Through an examination of three Protestant church documents published in 2018, the essay goes on to show how more churches began to challenge populist rhetoric and also engage with the challenge of Christian-Muslim dialogue and the call for fresh Christian theological engagements with Islam.

In the summer of 2015, European political and media discourse increasingly focused on the refugee crises caused by the Syrian war, as well as the ongoing turmoil in post-invasion Iraq and Afghanistan. Years earlier, millions of people had been forced to migrate from their homes and were living in refugee camps or in urban centres in Turkey, Jordan, and Lebanon. However, public and political attention on the severe challenge of forced migration was minimal until a large number of these people began to move into Europe to seek asylum and a new home. The migration crisis was suddenly both the most pressing political question and the dominant news story across Europe and North America. The initial responses to the movement of people were often sympathetic, drawing attention to our common humanity and the demands of political care enshrined in international law.¹ The heart-breaking image of Aylan Kurdi's dead body on the shores of Turkey quickly became a symbol of pain and tragedy of migration, eliciting compassion and calls for change.

Very quickly the political mood and social reality in Europe shifted. The Paris attacks of 2015, as well as other acts of violence in Berlin and Brussels, were connected, however tenuously, with refugees and immigrants. Similarly, the accounts of sexual harassment during the New Year's celebration in Cologne presented an image of refugees as a sexual threat. The original framing of migration as a humanitarian crisis transferred quickly to a debate about cultural belonging and religion, with refugees depicted as Muslim others who may be incapable of residing in Europe. Nicholas De Genova notes how the "figure of the refugee—so recently fashioned as an object of European compassion, pity, and protection—was refashioned with astounding speed" into the Muslim other who is a potential terrorist or criminal.²

There have been numerous academic studies that have examined the important function of rhetorical appeals to Christianity and Judeo-Christian values in the calls to protect Europe from immigrants, especially Muslims. Rogers Brubaker argues, for instance, that appeals to "Christianity have become increasingly central to national-populist rhetoric in the last decade."³ According to his analysis, the turn to Christianity is intricately tied up with Islam. Numerous nationalist populist parties in Western Europe have begun to construct a Christian-secular identity politics to resist the "civilizational threat from Islam."⁴ Christianity here does not function primarily as a set of religious practices or theological beliefs; in fact many who argue for this Judeo-Christian-Secular identity neither practice nor believe in traditional Christianity. Instead, Christianity serves as one central part in a broader imaginary of identity and civilisation that supports conceptions of freedom, gender equality, and liberalism. Christianism, as Brubaker names it, is juxtaposed with a depiction of Islam where freedom, gender equality, and political secularism are an impossibility.

While it may be tempting to dismiss these uses of Christianity as running against the teachings of the Church and the public statements of churches to care for migrants, this would be too simplistic. These ideas have a much longer lineage in the statements of theologians, practices of everyday Christians, and public rhetoric of Latin Christianity stretching back to at least the Crusades. Moreover, current Christians leaders and politicians from Viktor Orban and Archbishop Péter Erdö in Hungary to Swedish ministers have also interpreted the migration crisis as a sinister Muslim threat to Christianity and Europe.[5]

Agbonkhianmeghe Orobator, SJ argues that socio-political and economic crises present the church with a kairos moment, where God calls the community to respond with acts of faith and creativity. "A church that opts to engage" the socio-political and economic issues of its context "emerges as a church on a mission," moving "from crisis to kairos."[6] In an article written over three years ago, I argued that socio-political realities of migration and its public backlash present the churches in Europe with one such inter-religious kairos moment, demanding interfaith engagement. The challenge facing Christians in the West in responding to the migration crisis is in part to discover frameworks for Christian-Muslim engagement that resist presenting Christendom as locked in a recurring battle with the dar al-Islam. However, at the time the loudest theo-political reactions to the phenomenon of migration in Europe have been those that return to long standing tropes of inherent difference and cultural rivalry.[7]

This brief essay will reflect on one sign of hope in Christian-Muslim relations in the context of migration in Europe, especially in light of the increasing political restrictions against immigration and the rise of right wing nationalism. Hope can be found in the numerous pronouncements and ecclesial statements by Catholic, Protestant, and Orthodox churches calling for social care, political engagement, and church action to support migrants and refugees. While the initial pronouncements in 2015 focused very little on Islam and Muslims, as the situation continued and public rhetoric increasingly demonized Muslims migrants, more churches began to engage with the challenge of Christian-Muslim dialogue and to call for fresh Christian theological engagements with Islam.

In the summer of 2015 and into the autumn, churches and ecclesial leaders responded to movement of migrants into Europe with acts of hospitality. Churches were turned into makeshift processing centres. Christian aid groups were present on islands in Italy and Greece to welcome and aid the humans seeking refuge in Europe. Nearly every major church issued public pronouncements that called for care for migrants. Pope Francis, who had been a champion for immigrant and refugee rights for years before, demanded parishes across Europe welcome people seeking shelter.[8] Orthodox churches in Western Europe referenced their own histories of migration, and Patriarch Bartholomew insisted that Europe open its arms to people seeking new opportunities and life, using his Christmas sermons to connect Jesus' own birth and flight to Egypt with the current realities in Turkey, Syria, and Europe. Numerous Protestant denominations and national churches from Hungary to Scotland published public statements pointing to the biblical call to care for the migrant.

The documents were important, especially as they drew attention to the biblical calls to care for the least of these (Matt 25:40) and to treat the stranger as a citizen (Lev 19:34). However, the increasing fear of Muslims and demonization of migrants demanded more from churches. Even as Christianity was increasingly invoked as a tool against Muslims by the far-right and other politicians, many churches failed to challenge these claims directly but instead continued with general appeals to ethics or shared humanity. True signs of hope meet the challenge of the society and call of God directly. It is thus all the more urgent for Christians in the West to muster both the courage and humility to begin to risk genuine engagement with Muslims and to move beyond the fear and recrimination that has dominated most public and ecclesial debates. Until Christians confront our long and uneasy relationship with Muslims, we will remain caught between the dominant motifs of fear and nostalgia that cling to a past Christian Europe or simplistic accounts of tolerance that calls for a generic love of neighbour but fails to address genuine difference. As such, the earlier church statements regarding care for the stranger needed to be advanced to include more indepth reflection on Christian-Muslim relations as well as the specific legal, political, and social challenges in Europe and within each country.

Given my own location as a Protestant theologian, I will turn to three such documents from 2018 that Protestant churches in Europe issued, each calling for increased engagement with Islam and Christian-Muslim dialogue.[9] These mark a shift from 2015 when the churches' public statements focused primarily on care for the stranger in the abstract without any specific focus on Islam or Muslims. The 2018 documents evidence stances that engage more concretely with Muslims and see churches challenging the rising xenophobia and anti-Muslim rhetoric in Europe. They also show how the socio-political and cultural challenges of migration pressed Christian theology and churches to think afresh about Islam.

The first comes from the World Communion of Reformed Churches (WCRC) European meeting in Budapest, Hungary in April of 2018. The WCRC in Europe includes 40 member churches in 29 countries that represent around 80 million people coming from the Reformed, Congregational, Presbyterian, United, and Waldensian Community. The 2018 gathering in Budapest occurred a few days after the Hungarian election, which provided a resounding majority to the right wing populist prime minister Viktor Orbán, himself a member of the Reformed church in Hungary. The campaign relied heavily on anti-migrant rhetoric and presented Orbán as a protector of Hungary and broader Christian European values. Within this context, the churches gathered to reflect on the work of its task force on migration in Europe and to hear recommendations about future work.[10] In addition to calling for more diaconal care, social integration, and advocacy, the WCRC called attention to the importance of attending to Christian-Muslim relations, both politically and theologically.

Politically the document noted how Christianity and Islam were deployed in anti-migrant discourse. "The rise of many far-right parties that praise European culture and Judeo-Christian values do so in the name of rejecting human beings who are seeking refugee or a new life…. The WCRC and its member churches have continually issued public statements and raised alternative voices to these."[11] In response, the WCRC asked for more theological engagement with Islam and an increased role for Christian-Muslim dialogue. The main action point, which was unanimously approved, was for the churches "to improve Christian-Muslim relations by increasing cooperation and dialogue with the Middle East partners of the WCRC, and also learning from the experiences of other WCRC European partners in their cooperation with Muslims."[12] While the WCRC's statement issued a call for increased Christian-Muslim dialogue and fresh theological reflection on Islam, it did not offer much of it. Two documents issued later in the same year in Germany do move in these directions. The first presents a more political reflection on Christian-Muslim dialogue, while the second moves in a more distinctly theological direction.

Migration as a Kairos Moment for Protestant-Muslim Dialogue

In September of 2018, the Evangelische Kirche in Deutschland (EKD), a confederation that includes Lutheran, Reformed, and United churches in Germany and thus represents the majority of Protestants in the country, issued a new position paper on the urgent need for Christian-Muslim relations and fresh political theological reflection on Islam. The document opens by recognising the co-humanity and shared citizenship of Christians and Muslims in Germany, grounding this in the German basic law and an account of the Holy Spirit's presence in the world. The church goes on to confess that the Protestant churches in Germany struggled to "recognise religious plurality," but now affirms religious diversity in the country and seeks to treat "Muslims with respect and appreciation, regardless of the different claims of revelation and truth between Christianity and Islam."[13]

The most promising aspect of the document is the way that it calls for a spirit of non-hostile recognition of difference within the public square. Challenging ardent secularists who envision the privatisation of religion and some Christians who seek financial support from the government and religious freedom only for themselves, the churches support a dynamic political pluralism grounded in mutual respect, justice, and freedom. For the EKD, the secular state of Germany is one that is religiously neutral and affords political equality before the law to all religions. Given this legal tradition in Germany, especially towards the Catholic and Protestant communities, "The Evangelical Church is keen to ensure that Muslims and their organizational forms in Germany are able to work freely and to participate in the opportunities for development in the public square."[14] To accomplish this demands openness and adaptability from the German national government, the 16 *Bundesländer*, from churches, and also from Muslim communities. It honestly names how segments of society, including church members, harbour suspicions against all Muslims and question their presence in Germany and Europe. The churches note the reality of violence carried out by Muslims, but warns "against hastily coming to general and general conclusions where differentiation and differentiation are required."[15] There is much left unsaid in this document, but we begin to see the sketches of a vision of European Christianity that both values its unique political contributions and history, but also seeks to extend these social privileges outward to include others, especially Muslims.

A more intentionally theological document was published in the Autumn of 2018 by the *Evangelische Kirche im Rheinland*, a United Protestant church consisting of both Lutheran and Reformed traditions.[16] The position paper was an advancement of an earlier document from 2015 that initiated engagement with Muslims and sought a theological basis for dialogue. In addition to a number of important ethical claims focused on the church's rejection of racism, anti-Semitism, and Islamophobia, the majority of the document focused on theological and scriptural reasons for dialogue with Muslims. The fact that the church wrote and debated a fairly nuanced theological statement on Islam illustrates the ways that the situation of migration in Europe in general and in Germany more specifically served as a dramatic impetus for fresh theological engagement.

In the document, the church sketches out the contours of a Protestant theological engagement with Islam, one that draws on scripture, the Protestant tradition, and also Vatican II, while learning from its previous failings in Christian-Jewish relations. Two central theological ideas stand out. The first is how it locates Islam within the broader biblical tradition, albeit not necessarily in the Old and New Testament as such. Islam is presented as part of a Scriptural and Abrahamic trialogue and thus Muslims have a special relationship with Christians. This relationship is analogous to Judaism, although not the same. Jews and Christians share and debate the Hebrew Bible, while Muslims do not and look to the Qur'an as the revelation of God. Islam is thus secondary to the constitutive relationship with Judaism, but it remains important and requires distinct areas of dialogue and theological reflection.[17] By making this distinction between Christian-Jewish and Christian-Muslim relations, the church does not intend to exclude Muslims from the biblical traditions. Instead, the authors affirm a broader shared heritage, especially related to a confession of the one God and common figures like Abraham, which link Muslims and Christians.

The second theologically vital component of the document is its focus on Jesus Christ, not as a means to reject Muslims or Islam, but as grounding for dialogical exchange. This is justified in a few ways. First, the second section begins by categorically stating that "Christians who hold fast to their commitment to the truth of Jesus Christ can also perceive in Islam, God's history with human beings."[18] The fact that Christians and Muslims disagree over the salvific importance of Jesus, as well as his relationship to the divine nature, is not sufficient reason to reject Muslim claims to worship the one God. Just as Jesus engaged with people from a variety of perspectives and contexts, so too should Christians. Moreover, the church interprets Romans 9 as stating that God's activity extends beyond the knowledge and confessions of the church. Building on these scriptural and theological groundings, the document concludes that Christian-Muslim dialogue is a church mandate and one to be carried out in a spirit of openness and faith

The theological questions that Islam presents to Christianity cannot be ignored, but must be engaged in ways that attend to history, scripture, and the contemporary reality. Rather than rely on old tropes that demonize Muslims or view Muhammad as religious imposter, the church calls for serious theological consideration of Islam from a Christian perspective. In so doing the church affirms its own central commitments to Jesus Christ, but also recognises God's presence with Muslims in the history of Islam. The document is far from a fully developed theological reflection on the many thorny theological challenges of Christian-Muslim dialogue, but it does represent an invitation for further reflection and debate on how to understand the church's dual commitments to faith in Jesus Christ and openness to God's active presence with Muslims.

Taken together, these three documents, as well as others written over the past five years, illustrate how the questions and challenges of migration are pressing Christians to engage more concretely with Muslims. Over the last years, numerous sites of hope can also be discerned through the actions of individuals and communities. These less visible acts of hospitality and social resistance find Christians, Muslims, and other people of faith or no religious faith enacting the truth of our common humanity, defying death dealing policies, and offering an alternative to the rhetoric of an inherent clash of religions. German pastors and priests are using centuries old laws about asylum to protect refugees from deportation. Catholic and Waldensian Christians are gathering together in Lampedusa to mourn and lament the deaths of human beings in the sea, all while calling for new just laws and safe corridors. Syrian Muslim who have been resettled in the United Kingdom are volunteering in hospitals to help during the Covid-19 pandemic. These acts of inter-religious human solidarity advance the public statements of the churches and cultivate human dignity by calling forth a "dangerous memory" that disrupts the political fixation on citizenship status, borders, and political management. It is in these lived realities, which the public statements of churches can only witness to, that we see further signs of lasting hope grounded in human solidarity.

Nostra Aetate §3's call for Christians and Muslims to move beyond the rivalry and violence of centuries and "to forget the past" and work for "social justice and moral welfare, as well as peace and freedom" remains a prophetic call to Christians, both Catholics and others. Protestant theologians and churches in Europe have lagged behind the Catholic church in engaging seriously with both Islam and Muslims. The last few years have seen Protestant churches in Europe increasingly take up the Vatican's call for engagement. And yet the invitation to forget the past seems overly optimistic, when the past remains a vital force in the political, social, and theological imaginary of public, political, and popular discourse. For instance, the Ottoman advance on Vienna and conquests of south-eastern Europe have been invoked by politicians in Hungary and right-wing nationalist movements across Europe as justification for closing borders and treating all Muslims, be the citizens or immigrants, with suspicion. Those Christians who wish to resist the rise of Christianism must not simply forget the past, but engage with it through honest evaluations of our failings, repentance for our sins, and thereby engage the work of theological repair. Only then, will Christian-Muslim dialogue be able to sustain the shared work of social justice and moral welfare. There remains much work to be done, but the theological and ecclesial reflection examined in this essay are signs of hope that might seed an alternative future for Christian-Muslim relations in Europe.

Notes

1. Most prominently the United Nations' 1951 Convention Relating to the Status of Refuges and the 1967 Protocol Relating to the Status of Refugees.
2. Nicholas De Genova (ed.), *The Borders of 'Europe': Autonomy of Migration, Tactics of Bordering*, Durham: Duke University Press, 2017, 17.
3. Rogers Brubaker, "Between nationalism and civilizationism: the European populist moment in comparative perspective," Ethnic and Racial Studies 40 (2017),1191-1926, here 1198.
4. Brubaker, "Between nationalism and civilizationism," here, 1193.

5. Johanna Gustafsson Lundberg, "Christianity in a Post-Christian Context: Immigration, Church Identity, and the Role of Religion in Public Debate," in Ulrich Schmiedel and Graeme Smith (eds.), *Religion in the European Refugee Crisis* (Palgrave, 2018), 123-124.
6. Agbonkhianmeghe E. Orobator, *From Crisis to Kairos: The Mission of the Church in the Time of HIV/AIDS*, Nairboi: Paulines Publications Africa, 2005, 18.
7. Joshua Ralston, "Bearing Witness: Reframing Christian-Muslim encounter in light of the refugee crisis," *Theology Today* 74 (2017), 22-35, here 26.
8. For instance in his first apostolic exhortation, *Evangelii Gaudium*, Pope Francis noted how "Migrants present a particular challenge for me, since I am the pastor of a Church without frontiers, a Church which considers herself mother to all. For this reason, I exhort all countries to a generous openness which, rather than fearing the loss of local identity, will prove capable of creating new forms of cultural synthesis. How beautiful are those cities which overcome paralysing mistrust, integrate those who are different and make this very integration a new factor of development." §210
9. Given the Catholic Church's long commitment to engagement with Muslims since the second Vatican Council, the Church has a much longer tradition of theological reflection upon Islam and dialogical engagement with Muslims.
10. I served on this task force from 2016-2018 along with ministers and lay leaders from Italy, Sweden, Greece, Hungary, and Germany. As the lone academic theologian, I primarily drafted the document with input from the rest of the steering committee, especially the sections highlighting national work.
11. "When God recommends guest and sojourners to them…": *The Church's Mission and Work in the Context of Migration*, 29-30 https://www.wcrc-europe.eu/%2C%2CWhen_God_recommends_guests_and_sojourners_to_them_...-20219-0-0-26.html
12. Ibid., 32.
13. Positionspapier der EKD zum christlich-islamischen Dialog https://www.ekd.de/positionspapier-der-ekd-zum-christlich-islamischen-dialog-37797.htm
14. Ibid.
15. Ibid.
16. *Für die Begegnung mit Muslimen. Theologische Positionsbestimmung*, http://www.ekir.de/www/downloads/DS30FuerdieBegegnungmitMuslimen.pdf
17. *Für die Begegnung mit Muslimen. Theologische Positionsbestimmung*, 4. http://www.ekir.de/www/downloads/DS30FuerdieBegegnungmitMuslimen.pdf
18. *Für die Begegnung mit Muslimen. Theologische Positionsbestimmung*, 5.

Part Two: Hope in Sacrifice and Solidarity

Monastic-Muslim Dialogue

WILLIAM SKUDLAREK

Some fifty years ago, Cardinal Sergio Pignedoli formally invited monks to become more involved in interreligious dialogue, arguing that monasticism is "a bridge connecting all religions." In 1995, Dom Christian de Chergé, prior of Notre Dame de l'Atlas monastery in Algeria, argued for the expansion of monastic dialogue to include Muslims, describing how monastics could benefit from and contribute to this dialogue. In addition to local Monastic-Muslim encounters for dialogue since that time, there has been an on-going dialogue of Catholic monastics with Iranian Shi'a Muslims since 2011. The future holds promise for an expansion of Monastic-Muslim dialogue in Africa.

In May 1995, Christian de Chergé, prior of Notre Dame de l'Atlas, a Trappist monastery near the village of Tibhirine in Algeria, spoke at the annual meeting of the European Commission of Dialogue Interreligieux Monastique·Monastic Interreligious Dialogue (DIM·MID). He had been invited to describe his experience of dialogue with Muslims and to explain why it was appropriate for monks to be involved in dialogue with the followers of a religious tradition that does not include an institutionalized form of monasticism. His lecture and example laid the groundwork for the major role that Monastic-Muslim dialogue plays in the mission of DIM·MID today.

I Christian de Chergé

Christian de Chergé was born in 1937, one of eight children of a distinguished French family. His first experience of Algeria came in his early childhood. His family lived there for three years during the Second

World War when his father, a general in the French army, was in command of an artillery regiment. One of his older brothers recalled that young Christian was impressed by the way Muslims prayed, and that their mother assured him that Muslims prayed to the same God we did.

Christian's love for Algeria and for Islam matured when he returned to fulfil his compulsory military service some twenty years later, during the time of the country's war of independence. In the village where he was posted he became friends with a certain Mohammed, a rural policeman and father of ten. On one occasion as they were conversing they were confronted by members of the FLN, the National Liberation Front. When one of them pointed his gun at Christian, Mohammed stood between them and said, "This is a good man; do not harm him." After the partisans dispersed, Christian, realizing the risk that Mohammed had taken, told him he would pray for him. Mohammed graciously accepted his offer, but could not help observing that "Christians don't really know how to pray."

That night Mohammed was killed. The fact that a devout Muslim gave his life for him deeply moved Christian and reinforced his desire to become a priest. When he returned to France, he continued the seminary studies he had begun before being drafted into the army and was then ordained in 1964. In 1969, after spending four years as a school chaplain in Paris, he entered the Trappist abbey of Aiguebelle in southeastern France with the intention of joining the community in Algeria.

De Chergé arrived at the monastery of Our Lady of Atlas in 1971. In order to prepare for his life as a monk in a Muslim country, he spent the next two years at the Pontifical Institute for Arabic and Islamic Studies (PISAI) in Rome. He then returned to Algeria and ten years later, in 1984, the monastic community elected him to be the superior. The regular spiritual conferences he gave to his community, as well as those he gave to religious communities throughout Algeria, show how much he was indebted to the Qur'an and to Muslim authors for his understanding of God, of prayer, and of the spiritual life in general.

Even though de Chergé devoted himself to the study of Islam and its relation to Christian revelation, interreligious dialogue with Algerian Muslims was not primarily an intellectual exercise for him and for other members of the Tibhirine community. Their dialogue with Muslims mainly occurred in two different settings. First there was a "dialogue of life" that consisted of monks working side by side with their neighbours in the agricultural cooperative organized by the monastery, attending to them in the monastery's clinic, and even taking part in their family celebrations. There was also a "dialogue of spiritual experience" that took place in one-to-one encounters and in meetings of the *Ribāt es Salām*, "the bond of peace," which de Chergé helped to found. The members of this Islamo-Christian group met twice a year, not for theological discussions, but to share with one another in a prayerful setting what they had experienced over the previous six months as they reflected on a particular theme that was common to both religions.

When he spoke to the European DIM·MID delegates at the Benedictine Abbey of Montserrat in 1995, Algeria was in the middle of a decade-long war between the government and various Islamic rebel organizations. On the night of March 26-27, 1996, less than a year after he had spoken at Montserrat, he and six of his brother monks were kidnapped and then killed two months later. His last will and testament, which he had sent to his mother two years earlier to be opened in the event he should lose his life, offers moving testimony to the spiritual riches he discovered and cherished through his encounters with devout Muslims.[1]

II The Presentation of Christian de Chergé

We do not have the text of the address de Chergé gave to the European delegates of DIM·MID in 1985, but we do have a record of what he said based on his notes and notes taken by a participant.[2] These notes show that he was well aware that the primary purpose of DIM·MID from its founding in 1978 was to promote inter-monastic dialogue. Recognizing that monasticism as an institution does not exist in Islam and that very few Christian monks had engaged in dialogue with Muslims, he still believed that there were at least four reasons why Monastic-Muslim dialogue would be fully in harmony with the mission of DIM·MID to promote dialogue at the level of spiritual practice and experience.

First of all, while it is true that some passages in the Qur'ān are critical of monks - Surah 9:34, for example, speaks of "many among the priests and anchorites, who in falsehood devour the substance of men and hinder (them) from the way of Allah"[3] — there are other passages that are quite positive.

The first example de Chergé gives is the "light verse" from Surah 24:

> Allah is the Light of the heavens and the earth. The parable of His Light is as if there were a Niche, and within it a Lamp: the Lamp enclosed in Glass . . . Light upon Light! Allah guides who He will to His Light. . . (Lit is such a Light) in houses, which Allah has permitted to be raised to honour; for the celebration, in them, of His name: in them is He glorified in the mornings and in the evenings, (again and again) (35-36).[4]

The clearest Qur'anic expression of a positive regard for monks is to be found in Surah 5:82:

> [N]earest . . . in love to the Believers will you find those who say, "We are Christians": because amongst these are men devoted to learning and men who have renounced the world, and they are not arrogant.[5]

Having established that monks and monasticism are not foreign to the Qur'ān, de Chergé then goes on to speak of three significant links between Islam and the monastic tradition. He draws a connection between the central place of obedience in the monastic tradition and the importance of surrender or submission in Islam. Secondly, the monastic practice of coming together several times a day for common prayer (*opus Dei*) parallels the Muslim practice of daily ritual prayer (*salāt*). Finally the monastic practice of *lectio divina*, the meditative reading of Sacred Scripture as God's word directed to the reader, is echoed by the Muslim conviction that in and through the Qur'ān, God speaks to each individual. This conviction is most clearly evident in the "Night of Power" during the final days of Ramadan when Muslims believe a verse of the Qur'ān can descend upon a believer as a word personally directed to that individual.

De Chergé maintained that monastic dialogue with Muslims should be distinguished by spiritual sharing rather than by dogmatic considerations. Since Islam is a religion "penetrated with monastic values," he suggests that Monastic-Muslim dialogue address such topics as the invocation of the Name, monotheism, the way of Jesus, the desire for God, the gift of prophecy, and submission to God.

In the previous year, in an address to the general chapter of the Trappists, de Chergé had expanded on the kind of dialogue that takes into account the "monastic values" of Islam:

> . . . there are those values that animate Islam and which we also ordinarily expect to find among monks: ritual prayer, prayer of the heart (*dhikr*), fasting, vigils, almsgiving, a sense of praise and of God's forgiveness, a naked faith in the glory of the Wholly Other, and in the communion of saints. This last mystery, so essential to us, reveals a place of encounter, but [gives] no idea of how we can get there. It belongs to the Spirit of Jesus to do His work among us, and I feel that in this process, He also uses our differences, including those which offend us most. In our prayer side by side with our Sufi friends, which we have now been at for quite a while, we remind ourselves that [together] we are following a "way," a *tariqa*, . . . [that is] "ordered" to an active and passive search in a mysticism of desire leading to union with God. The spiritual competition then becomes mutual charity, common evidence that we are being drawn in the same direction.[6]

De Chergé concluded his presentation at the DIM·MID meeting by emphasizing the role of hospitality, not only in welcoming Muslim guests to the monastery, but in welcoming their culture and their spirituality. Quoting from Surah 5:48, he reiterates his conviction that it is precisely our differences that keep us in relationship and stimulate us in our common quest for unity in God:

> Had Allah willed, He would have made you one nation [united in religion], but [He intended] to test you in what He has given you; so race to [all that is] good. To Allah is your return all together, and He will [then] inform you concerning that over which you used to differ.

De Chergé poignantly expresses that conviction in his last will and testament when he says that if he should be killed,

> my avid curiosity will then be satisfied. This is what I shall be able to do, if God wills - immerse my gaze in that of the Father, and contemplate with him his children of Islam just as he sees them, all shining with the glory of Christ, the fruit of His Passion, and filled with the Gift of the Spirit, whose secret joy will always be to establish communion and to refashion the likeness, playfully delighting in the differences.[7]

III Monastic-Muslim Dialogue with Shi'a Muslims

In spite of the de Chergé's moving appeal for monks to enter wholeheartedly into dialogue with Muslims, it took some time for that appeal to be translated into action. Individual monasteries began reaching out to local Muslims communities, especially after the terrorist attacks of September 11, 2001, but it was only in 2011 that DIM·MID began organizing formal Monastic-Muslim dialogue, inaugurating a series of dialogues with Shi'a Muslims that has continued to the present day.

The origins of this dialogue go back to England in the late 1990s when an Iranian doctoral student, Mohammad Ali Shomali,[8] was pursuing a degree in philosophy at the University of Manchester. When he told a Catholic priest he had met that he wanted to take advantage of his time in England to learn more about Christianity and asked how he could go about visiting a Catholic seminary, the priest, who was a monk of Ampleforth, introduced him to his abbot, Timothy Wright. Shomali and Wright soon became friends, and Wright invited Shomali to speak to the monastic community. Shomali, in turn, invited Wright to Qum, where he lectured at the Imam Khomeini Education and Research Institute.

During that visit, Wright and Shomali discussed the possibility of holding a Catholic-Shi'a conference at Ampleforth. The meeting took place in 2003 with the involvement of Heythrop College, London, and focused on questions of spirituality and theology in the two traditions. Two more conferences followed, the second in 2005 on reason and faith, and the third in 2007 on ethics.[9]

In 2010, at the request of Shomali and Wright, DIM·MID assumed sponsorship for the Catholic part of this dialogue, and in 2011 the first specifically Monastic-Muslim dialogue was held in Rome. Subsequent dialogues took place in 2012 (Qom/Isfahan), 2014 (Assisi/Rome), 2016 (Qom/Mashhad), 2017 (Nairobi), and 2019 (London/Ampleforth). The topics for these dialogues were monastic and Shi'a spirituality, friendship, community, human dignity, unity of God and unity in God, and mission/conversion.[10] The next Monastic-Muslim dialogue is scheduled for Vienna in 2020 on the topic of suffering and martyrdom.

IV Characteristics of Monastic-Muslim Dialogue

As the topics chosen for these meetings indicate, DIM·MID in its dialogue with Shi'a Muslims has followed de Chergé's counsel and focused on spiritual sharing rather than academic discussions of dogma. By choosing friendship as the topic of the second dialogue, we also recognized the key role that the friendship of Timothy Wright and Mohammad Ali Shomali played in initiating this dialogue and how important it is that those who participate in these encounters become friends if their exchanges are to be open and mutually enriching.

Dogmatic questions, of course, cannot be completely avoided. That was especially true of the dialogue devoted to the unity of God and unity in God. However, the goal of that particular dialogue was not to compare, much less debate, dogmatic formulations about the existence and nature of God, but to provide a space in which we could speak openly to one another about how our faith in the One God motivates us to work for unity, whether that be within our own communities of faith, with people of other faiths, or within society at large.

We approached the topic of the oneness of God heedful of de Chergé's observation that "To speak of things in a different way does not mean that one is speaking of different things. Likewise, to speak of God in a different way does not mean that there is another [God], but that God is Utterly Other—in other words, different from everything that is."[11] At the end of our dialogue on the unity of God and unity in God, one of the Muslim participants said that he did not agree with his co-religionists who believed that Christians were polytheists. "You share our belief in One God," he said, "but the way you express your faith in the Oneness of God is Trinitarian." He added that while he did not agree with this way of speaking of the Oneness of God, he accepted the honesty and sincerity of Christians who said that belief in the Trinity did not weaken or compromise their belief in the Unity of God.

A central feature of Monastic-Muslim dialogue is that time for prayer is an integral part of our gatherings. Meetings hosted by DIM·MID take place in a monastery and our discussions are scheduled around the times the monastic community prays the Liturgy of Hours and the Eucharist. The set times for *salāt* are also incorporated into the schedule of all our meetings. The monastic participants are welcome to join the Muslims at their times for prayer, and the Muslims to join the monastics for their liturgical services.

V Looking to the Future

As we look to the future of Monastic-Muslim dialogue, our eyes are turned especially to Africa. According to the on-line OSB Atlas, on this continent, which is about 50% Muslim, there are nearly 100 abbeys, priories, and houses of Benedictine monks and nuns. Two of these communities have over 100 members, three have between 50 and 99 members, and eleven have between 15 and 19. In addition, Africa has 32 Cistercian monasteries.

There are two particular reasons to be hopeful about the future of Monastic-Muslim dialogue in Africa. A Kenyan Benedictine monk who has taken part in all but one of DIM·MID's dialogue with Shi'a Muslims has recently successfully defended his doctoral dissertation at PISAI, the school where de Chergé studied for two years and deepened his appreciation for and love of the Muslim *tariqa*.

Secondly, at the Monastic-Muslim dialogue that took place in Nairobi in 2017, two half-day sessions on the unity of God and unity in God were held at Tangaza University College, a constituent college of the Catholic University of Eastern Africa. As a follow-up to the success of these sessions, it was decided that in conjunction with the International Institute for Islamic Studies in Iran, Tangaza would each year organize a conference on the same topic and a three-week course on "Islam and Christianity in Dialogue". Planning was also begun to expand the academic program to include a BA in Islamic Studies and Christian-Muslim Relations that would examine the specific dimensions of Islam in Africa and the relations and dialogue between Christians and Muslims worldwide.

On November 1, 2019, Tangaza formally inaugurated the Institute for Interreligious Dialogue and Islamic Studies (IRDIS), which in addition to offering the above-mentioned BA, will also facilitate specialization in Islamic studies in existing MA and PhD programs, organize meetings and conferences, design trainings and summer courses, etc.

Given the role that DIM·MID played in the establishment of IRDIS, Tangaza University College has expressed its eagerness to have DIM·MID actively contribute to its new programs in Islamic Studies. *In shā' Allāh*, through DIM·MID's collaboration with IRDIS, the seed planted by Christian de Chergé in Algeria will continue to grow and produce rich fruit throughout Africa and beyond.

Notes

1. The testament is easily accessible online.
2. 'Y a-t-il une connivence monastique possible entre Christianisme et Islam?' Bulletin de la commission francophone, 14 (June 1996) 3-6.
3. *The Qur'ān*, trans. Abdullah Yusuf Ali, Elmhurst NY, Tahrike Tsarsile Qur'ān, Inc., 2001. Subsequent citations from the Qur'ān will also be from this translation.
4. Cosmas Hoffmann, coordinator of the European Commissions of DIM·MID, points out that even in pre-Islamic poetry one can find the image of *rāhib*, the monk who lives in the desert. The "light verse" of this Surah may well be be an allusion to the light that comes from the oil lamp in the niche of a *rāhib's* cell and promises shelter for travelers. See C. Hoffmann, 'Wertschätzung und Abgrenzung: Mönche im Koran und im Islam,' Erbe und Auftrag, 3/19 (August 2019), 248. This issue of Erbe und Auftrag was devoted to the theme "Mönchtum und Islam."
5. This passage was quoted by de Chergé to Sayah Attia, the leader of a group of rebels who came to the monastery on Christmas Eve 1993 demanding medical care for a wounded comrade. "Of Gods and Men" (Des dieux et des hommes), the award-winning film from the year 2010, dramatizes the scene by having de Chergé begin the verse in French and Attia finish it in Arabic.
6. Christian de Chergé, "Conference Given to General Chapter of Trappist Order," *Monastic Interreligious Dialogue Bulletin*, 55 (Spring 1996) 20.
7. My emphasis.
8. Dr Shomali is Director of the International Institute for Islamic Studies in Qum, Iran, which he founded in 2009, and former Head of the Islamic Centre of England, London.
9. The proceedings, originally published by Melisende (London) in 2004, 2006, and 2008, were reissued in paperback in 2011. Vol. I, *Catholics and Shi'a in Dialogue*; Vol. II, *A Catholic Shi'a Encounter*; Vol. III, *A Catholic- Shi'a Dialogue*.
10. The proceedings of the 2011, 2012, and 2014 meetings were edited by Mohammed Shomali and Willliam Skudlarek: *Monks and Muslims: Monastic and Shi'a Spirituality in Dialogue*, Collegeville MN, Liturgical Press, 2012; *Monks and Muslims II: Creating Communities of Friendship*, Collegeville MN, Liturgical Press, 2014; and *Monks and Muslims III: Towards a Global Abrahamic Community*, London: Institute of Islamic Studies, 2015. Extensive reports on these and subsequent dialogues can be found in Dilatato Corde, the on-line journal of DIM·MID at www.dimmid.com.
11. Christian de Chergé, *L'invincible espérance*, Paris, Bayard, 1997, p. 127. My translation/paraphrase of "Mais voir les choses différemment ne signifie pas qu'on ne voit pas les mêmes choses. De même, quand Dieu se dit autrement, il ne se dit pas autre, mais Tout-Autre, c'est-à-dire autrement que tous les autres. "

Martyrdom and Hope in Muslim-Christian Dialogue

CHRISTIAN S. KROKUS

Is martyrdom a sign of hope in Muslim-Christian dialogue? In his Testament, Christian de Chergé insists that his life would be given to God and for his Muslim neighbours, not taken. His approach, which appropriates Jeanne de Chantal's category martyrdom of love emphasizes daily acts of service and surrender both within the monastery and among Muslim neighbours. The witness of Tibhirine provides some indication for how one might understand extraordinary suffering and death neither naïvely nor cynically but as communication of theological hope, and has been continued by the likes of Paolo Dall'Oglio, Frans Van der Lugt, and Jacques Murad.

At a memorial service on 26 May 1996, when it became known that the seven Trappist monks of Notre Dame d'Atlas at Tibhirine, Algeria had been killed, Jean-Marie Lustiger, the cardinal archbishop of Paris remarked: "Their death must be a sign of hope, that love is stronger than hatred."[1] The monks, whose story has received worldwide attention through the film *Of Gods and Men*, were beatified by Pope Francis as martyrs along with Bishop Pierre Claverie and eleven other Catholic victims of the Algerian civil war. They were beloved by their Muslim neighbours, but as the violence increased around them, and when the rebels began to target foreigners in particular, the monks were counselled either to accept military protection or to leave Algeria. They described themselves as birds on a branch, between staying and taking flight, but a Muslim neighbour pleaded: "But we are the birds, and you are the branch. If you depart, we have nowhere to go."² How can the martyrdom of these men be considered a sign of hope, whose deaths robbed a village of its spiritual support and the Algerian Church of its "lungs," as the archbishop emeritus of Algiers, Cardinal Duval, described the monastery?³ The Christian monks were murdered by Muslim men; how can their martyrdom communicate hope for Muslim-Christian dialogue?

Although he did not ask those questions in exactly those terms, Christian de Chergé, the prior of Notre Dame d'Atlas, reflected in his last years on the meaning of the monks' impending martyrdom and how it would be interpreted by others. In his later writings, amidst rising instability, fear, and violence, de Chergé emphasized a martyrdom of love, a patient, humble, constant, ordinary, giving of oneself in love to God and neighbour. His approach provides some clues about how martyrdom might be understood as a sign of hope in Muslim-Christian dialogue.⁴

I Martyrdom of love or *incarnation continuée*

De Chergé's understanding of martyrdom neither excludes nor emphasizes the traditional criterion of having been killed in *odium fidei* (hatred of the faith), but he expresses disapproval at "the hardness of some witnesses for the faith against their judges, at their confidence of being 'pure,' at their certitude that their persecutor will go straight to hell."⁵ Neither does his understanding cohere completely with contemporary efforts "to reconceptualize martyrdom as non-violent resistance to tyrannical rule."⁶ He worried that the designation of martyr could be weaponized: "Currently there are many 'martyrs' in our country. As much in one camp as in the other, each honours his dead under the glorious title of 'martyrs.'"⁷ Instead, rooted in the example of Jesus (John 10:17-18), de Chergé first emphasizes in his Testament that the martyr's life is given, not taken: "I would like my community, my Church and my family to remember that my life was GIVEN to God and to this country."⁸ Giving oneself to the other is an act of love; properly understood "the witness of Jesus, until his death, his 'martyrdom,' is a martyrdom of love."⁹

The expression martyrdom of love is usually associated with St. Maximillian Kolbe, but de Chergé attributed it primarily to an older source, St. Jeanne de Chantal. In his chapter-talks of 12 December (then her feast day) and 14 December 1995, de Chergé reports the following exchange between St. Jeanne and her Visitation nuns:

> My dear daughters, Saint Basil and most of the fathers and pillars of the church were not martyred. Why do you think this was so? [...] For myself, I believe that there is a martyrdom called the martyrdom of love in which God preserves the lives of His servants so that they might work for His glory. This makes them martyrs and confessors at the same time.

When asked about the length and status of such martyrdom, she responds:

> From the moment [...] when we have given ourselves up unreservedly to God until the moment when we die. [...] Don't concern yourself with their equality, [...] although I think there is little difference between them because "love is as strong as death," and martyrs of love suffer a thousand times more by staying alive to do God's will than if they had to give a thousand lives in witness of their faith, love and fidelity.[10]

St. Jeanne's martyrdom of love is the process by which one allows the heart of Jesus to reign in one's own heart. There is nothing triumphal about it. Such a martyrdom may remain hidden, and it must be practiced repeatedly. It may be more demanding than physical death, and it always builds up the other; it is never at his expense. De Chergé writes in his *Testament*: "I do not see, in fact, how I could rejoice if the people I love were indiscriminately accused of my murder. It would be too high a price to pay for what will perhaps be called, the 'grace of martyrdom' to owe it to an Algerian, whoever he might be, especially if he says he is acting in fidelity to what he believes to be Islam."[11] De Chergé loves Algeria and Islam, which he refers to respectively as "a body and a soul," and he refers even to the person who would kill him as his "last-minute friend."[12] One simply cannot rejoice if one's beloved is scorned.

De Chergé's 1994 Holy Thursday homily opens by contemplating the events surrounding the last supper: "Washing of feet, the shared cup and bread, the cross... a single commandment of love, a single WITNESS. This is the witness of Jesus, his 'testament,' in Greek "martyrion," the 'martyrdom' of Jesus."[13] Jesus' martyrdom is identified primarily with humble service to his friends. For de Chergé the various moments of Jesus' life cannot be separated from each other, nor any of it separated from the incarnation of the divine Word. The birth of Jesus is the incarnation of the Son, but no more so than the years at Nazareth during which Jesus was developing physically, psychologically, and spiritually, no more so than the years of Jesus' public ministry, and no more so than his last days when he suffered and was killed: "What happened during the hours of the Passion is the Incarnation continued."[14] The reverse is also true. The earlier stages of Jesus' life, including the washing of his disciples' feet, already participate in his martyrdom. According to that logic, most of Jesus' martyrdom was neither dramatic nor noticed. It belonged, as Charles de Foucauld would say, to the hidden life of Nazareth, with family and at work. That was the point St. Jeanne made to her sisters, whose lives and deaths would remain hidden, and that is the point de Chergé emphasizes with his fellow Trappists. Even in the face of a dramatic end, they are called to the daily, ordinary, constant martyrdom of love preached by St. Jeanne.

De Chergé's chapter-talks were often devoted to the Order's Constitutions, which in good Christian-Muslim dialogical form he referred to as "our *shariâ*."[15] Reflecting on the lack of any mention therein of martyrdom, he wonders: "Is that because the monk must escape it, or never be exposed to it?" He answers: "It is perhaps because it does not add anything substantial to the dynamic of incarnation," which already includes participation in the cross, "itself of the everyday."[16] The monk is called to "give one's life for the love of God, in advance and unconditionally," but "those who have tried it know that this is really a true 'martyrdom' […]. It is the greater JIHÂD, the true combat of which the spiritual tradition of Islam speaks."[17] Lest anyone mistakenly think such martyrdom is easy:

> We know from experience that the small acts often count more, especially when they must be repeated each day. Washing the feet of his brothers that Holy Thursday passes, but what if it had to be done daily? And to all comers? When Fr. Bernardo tells us that the Order has more need of monks than of martyrs, obviously he was not speaking of this martyrdom that the monk effects in so many little ways. […] To put on an apron, as Jesus did, can be just as serious and solemn as the giving of one's life […] and vice versa, to give one's life can be just as simple as putting on an apron.[18]

Gestures of love can be especially difficult within a small community, where naturally "it is easier to give to this person than to that one, to love Brother so-and-so or Sister so-and-so rather than another one in the same community."[19] For de Chergé it is no accident that "the Prologue of the *Rule of St. Benedict* associates participation in the sufferings of Christ above all with the PATIENCE of living [monastic] stability joyously in the everyday."[20] Jesus' witness was universally one "of love for humanity, for all, even the thieves, even the assassins and the executioners, those who act in the darkness, ready to treat you like an animal that is to be slaughtered (Ps 49) or to torture you to death because one of yours became one of 'theirs.'" When the Emir Sayah Attiyah arrived at the monastery on Christmas Eve 1993 armed and demanding money, medicines, and that Frère Luc return with him to his camp, de Chergé refused, but he subsequently reflected: "If I have given my life to all Algerians, then I have given it also to the 'Emir' S.A. He does not take it from me."[21] When later he discovered the Emir was killed, de Chergé wrote:

> I know that he has slit the throats of one hundred forty-five people.... But I try to imagine his arrival in paradise after he died. It seems to me that beneath the gaze of our dear Lord I have the right to present three attenuating facts. First: as a matter of fact, he did not slit our throats; secondly: he left when I asked him to; and thirdly: after our conversation in the night, I told him, 'We are in the midst of preparations to celebrate Christmas, for us that is the birth of the Prince of Peace, and here you come in with weapons!' He replied, "I'm sorry, I didn't know."[22]

A martyrdom of love demands one release judgment and the psychological security of hating one's enemy, instead willing his good.

II Muslim-Christian dialogue

In the specific context of Tibhirine, a martyrdom of love meant in the first place adopting what Stephanie Saldaña calls a "theology of staying put."[23] Counseled by many to leave, the monks ultimately followed the advice of Cardinal Duval who preached 'CONSTANCY' and who saw the Church's Algerian mission as one of "presence, prayer, and sharing" in the suffering of the people.[24] It also meant refusing to take sides in a conflict between different groups of Muslims, "not in order to take refuge in neutrality so that we can wash our hands of things – which is impossible – but in order to remain free to *love* all, because that is our choice, in the name of Jesus and with his grace."[25] Hence the monks referred to government soldiers as "brothers of the plain" and the Islamist rebels, whom others labelled "terrorists," as "brothers of the mountain."[26]

As established above, however, the monks' martyrdom did not begin with their decision to stay. It began with their original commitment to what de Chergé calls the "quasi-sacrament" of a "long living together" between Christians and Muslims.[27] Their martyrdom involved participating in formal dialogue, such as the semi-annual Muslim-Christian gatherings called *ribat as-salam* (bond of peace), and it involved many hours of informal dialogue between the monks and their Muslim friends and neighbours while labouring, praying, celebrating, and mourning together, for in those contexts the monks were forced to relinquish the caricatures and stereotypes of Muslims they may have held. De Chergé insisted those in dialogue keep "their feet on the ground (and even in the manure) but their heads seeking above."[28] His preferred image for dialogue is the mystical ladder, where the rails represent Christianity and Islam, and the rungs represent various spiritual practices and virtues. The ladder "is fixed in the earth, in the religious diversity in which we are immersed. It has its points of contact in God and the communion of saints."[29] Because it is possible to travel in either direction, as partners climb the rungs, they approach an eschatological communion of saints, but as they descend, together they birth through "labour pains" a Muslim-Christian communion of saints here and now.

A martyrdom of love demands serious study of Islam. De Chergé read the Qur'an according to the monastic practice of *lectio divina*, recognizing resonances between Qur'anic and Biblical passages and discovering therein a "short-cut to the Gospel." He surrendered uncritical claims of superiority and believed that Christians must learn something about God from Islam. When he read John Paul II's encyclical *Dives in Misericordia* in conversation with Qur'anic passages about mercy, he wondered: "Is it possible to speak in a Christian way about mercy without doing justice to all the 'keys' it plays in the hearts and religious traditions of humankind?

Are they aware in Rome that no Muslim can read the encyclical without feeling deeply ignored?"[30] If a Christian reader could approach the Qur'an with "a poor and disarmed heart, ready to listen to every word that comes from the mouth of the Most-High," then he might even recognize in Jesus the "true Muslim," the one who is all "yes" to the Father.[31]

Finally, in the everyday context of Muslim-Christian dialogue a disarmed heart recognizes that Christians do not exercise a monopoly on the martyrdom of love:

> We know from experience that the martyrdom of love is not the exclusive domain of Christians. We can receive this witness as a gift of the Spirit from anyone. Behind all the victims that the Algerian drama has already amassed, who can know how many authentic 'martyrs' of a simple and free love there are? One thinks of that man who the other day saved the life of a wounded policeman near Notre Dame d'Afrique. A few days later he paid with his own life. And the Bosnian Muslim who saved his fellow construction workers; he risked his own life too. From long ago, I cannot forget Muhammad, who one day protected my life by exposing his own [...] and who died, assassinated by his brothers because he refused to give them his friend. He could not choose between one or the other. *Ubi caritas...Deus ibi est!*[32]

For those with eyes to see, Christ's martyrdom of love infuses every aspect of human living with a paschal dimension to be appropriated whether knowingly or unknowingly.

III Martyrdom of hope?

In one of his last recorded chapter-talks, de Chergé notes that "our 'martyrdom' must be a 'martyrdom of love' and just as much a 'martyrdom of HOPE,' since everything is moving [...] toward the Kingdom of which the community is the image, though still not the full reality."[33] To ask whether martyrdom is a sign of hope in relation to Muslim-Christian dialogue is to ask whether the martyrdom in question provides for that context an experience of the Kingdom, whose foundational elements (from the Beatitudes) are love, acceptance, forgiveness, and sharing. De Chergé argues: "To the quip of our Abbot General that our Order needs monks more than martyrs, one must respond that we are truly monks by continuing to live here the very mystery of Christmas, of GOD LIVING with men... and thus by exposing ourselves, from the cradle, to the massacre of the Innocents."[34] Is such exposure to death a sign of God living among us? Is it the "self-sacrificing love," which according to Bernard Lonergan has the power to "liberate human reasonableness from its ideological prisons," to resist and reverse historical decline?[35] If, according to Servais Pinckaers, there is a "spirituality of martyrdom" such that one participates in the "pattern by which Christ's own death has transformed the world," the pattern will include not only Christ's physical death but his gift of self in love from birth onward.[36] Do we detect the pattern not only in the deaths but also in the lives of our martyrs? To the extent that we do, we also detect the continued incarnation of God, surely a sign of hope.

In the aftermath of the monks' kidnapping and execution, "thousands of ordinary Muslims responded to their death with letters of condolences and expressions of shame."[37] John Kiser concludes that "In retrospect, there were many signs that the monks' death had indeed been a turning point. For a country that seemed drunk on violence, their assassination in God's name was, for many Algerians, like hitting rock bottom. It was the final and highly publicized insult to an already-abused Islam."[38] Only a martyrdom of love makes possible the call of *Nostra Aetate* 3, which urges Christians and Muslims "to work sincerely for mutual understanding and to preserve as well as to promote together for the benefit of all humankind social justice and moral welfare, as well as peace and freedom."

Beyond death there is resurrection, perhaps even resurrection of the everyday. The violence has not ceased, but neither have the martyrdoms of love. In the context of the Syrian civil war for example, one thinks of Paolo Dall'Oglio, who founded a religious community devoted to dialogue with Muslims and was kidnapped in 2013 by ISIS, of Frans Van der Lugt, who cared for disabled Christians and Muslims, led young people on walks of friendship, and was killed in Homs during the siege of 2014, and of Jacques Murad who accompanied Dall'Oglio from the beginning, was kidnapped and tortured in 2015, escaped with the help of Muslim friends only to shepherd once again.[39] They were undoubtedly inspired by the Tibhirine seven to give themselves and to remain with their Christian and Muslim friends, not despite but because of the danger. Like de Chergé each would wish that we "associate [his] death [or capture] with so many other equally violent ones […] forgotten through indifference or anonymity."[40] If we understand death to include the ordinary, everyday, ongoing, and often anonymous martyrdom of love, whether in a Christian monastery or in a Muslim family, have we not detected the presence of God among us and therefore a reason to hope?

Notes

1. John Kiser, *The Monks of Tibhirine: Faith, Love, and Terror in Algeria*, New York: St. Martin's Press, 2002, 234. Unless from a secondary source, translations are mine. Usage of all caps is original to de Chergé.
2. Godefroy Roguenet de Saint-Albin, "Friendship in Tibhirine: Monastic/Muslim Dialogue in Algeria," in Mohammad Ali Shomali/William Skudlarek (eds.), *Monks and Muslims II: Creating Communities of Friendship*, Collegeville, MN: Liturgical Press, 2014, 19 n26.
3. Kiser, *Monks*, 4.
4. I apply only the Christian perspective. For majority/minority Islamic positions, see Asma Afsaruddin, "Competing Perspectives on Jihad and 'Martyrdom' in Early Islamic Sources," in Brian Wicker (ed.), *Witnesses to Faith?*, Aldershot: Ashgate, 2006, 15-32. For historical-theological analyses of martyrdom in Christian-Muslim contexts see Sidney Griffith, "Christians under Muslim Rule," in Thomas Noble and Julia Smith (eds.), *The Cambridge History of Christianity 3*, Cambridge: University of Cambridge Press, 2008, 197-212; Christian Sahner, *Christian Martyrs under Islam: Religious Violence and the Making of the Muslim World*, Princeton: Princeton University Press, 2018.
5. Christian de Chergé, *L'invincible espérance*, Montrouge: Bayard Éditions, 2010, 226.
6. Ruben Rodriguez Rosario, *Christian Martyrdom and Political Violence: A Comparative Theology with Judaism and Islam*, Cambridge: Cambridge University Press, 2017, 240.
7. De Chergé, *L'invincible*, 225.
8. Christian Salenson, *Christian de Chergé: A Theology of Hope*, translated from French by Nadia Conic (tr.), Collegeville, MN: Liturgical Press, 2012, 199.
9. De Chergé, *L'invincible*, 227.
10. Wendy Wright, *Bond of Perfection: Jeanne de Chantal & François de Sales*, Mahwah, NJ: Paulist Press, 1985, 154-55.
11. Salenson, *Theology*, 200.
12. Salenson, *Theology*, 201.
13. De Chergé, *L'invincible*, 225.
14. Christian de Chergé, *Dieu pour tout jour: Chapitres de Père Christian de Chergé à la communauté de Tibhirine (1986-1996)*, Montjoyer: Les Cahiers de Tibhirine, 2006, 542.
15. De Chergé, *Dieu*, 544.
16. De Chergé, *Dieu*, 545, 542.
17. De Chergé, *Dieu*, 546.
18. De Chergé, *L'invincible*, 228-29.
19. De Chergé, *L'invincible*, 229.

20. De Chergé, *Dieu*, 547.
21. De Chergé, *L'invincible*, 229.
22. Salenson, *Theology*, 173.
23. Stephanie Saldaña, "An Impossible Hope," *Plough Quarterly Magazine*, 13 (Summer 2017).
24. De Chergé, *Dieu*, 536; Kiser, *Monks*, 168.
25. De Chergé, *L'invincible*, 229, italics in original.
26. De Chergé, *L'invincible*, 316.
27. Salenson, *Theology*, 107.
28. Christian Salenson, *L'Échelle mystique du dialogue de Christian de Chergé*, Montrouge: Bayard Éditions, 2016: 22.
29. Salenson, *Theology*, 63.
30. Salenson, *Theology*, 43.
31. Salenson, *L'Échelle*, 51, 53.
32. De Chergé, *L'Invincible*, 230.
33. De Chergé, *Dieu*, 550.
34. De Chergé, *Dieu*, 539.
35. Bernard Lonergan, *Method in Theology*, New York: Seabury, 1979, 117.
36. Patrick Clark, "Translator's Preface" in Servais Pinckaers, *The Spirituality of Martyrdom...To the Limits of Love*, Patrick Clark/Annie Hounsokou (trs.), Washington, D.C.: Catholic University of America Press, 2016, xviii.
37. Kiser, *Monks*, 246.
38. Kiser, *Monks*, 258.
39. For an initial study of all three lives, see Saldaña, "Impossible."
40. Salenson, *Theology*, 199.

Part Three: Signs of Hope in Different Parts of the World

Signs of Hope for Christian-Muslim Relations in Indonesia

ALBERTUS BAGUS LAKSANA, S.J.

Contemporary Indonesian society is marked by a conservative turn among Muslims, both in the private and the public sphere that includes identity politics. This development has affected Christian-Muslim relations. In certain circles there is a growing sense of mutual alienation between the two communities. Yet this agonizing tension also begets an intense and concerted effort among mainstream Muslim organizations to push for a programmatic vision of an inclusive Islam within the framework of Indonesian nationalism as a platform for the common good. On their part, the Christian communities have also responded by developing more inclusive and contextual engagement with Muslims and other religious traditions through the framework of the common good and inclusive nationalism.

I Religion, Identity and Public Life
Hope is often born during the most difficult and testing time. In the past decade or so, Indonesian society has been in a more difficult and challenging situation. Roughly after the fall of the New Order regime (1998), Indonesia has been witnessing a dramatic change of the Islamic landscape in the country in connection with the larger global trend. After a period where political Islam was suppressed under the authoritarian New Order, diverse Islamic gro upings have entered politics with a sense of renewed purpose, often with the agenda of transforming society according to the purified ideals of Islam. Since then the public presence of political Islam has become more dominant within the framework of sectarian

identity politics.

In politics, the appeal and growth of conservative and transnational Islamic ideologies are quite real. New political parties are founded on, or are leaning toward, this kind of ideology as expressed in the Prosperous Justice Party (PKS), as well as other mass organizations that have gained political clout. In this context, we see a curious phenomenon since the Gubernatorial Election of Jakarta in 2017, namely, the metamorphosis of a mass movement, which was initially formed solely for the defence of the Muslim identity and Islamic political interests, into a mass organization. This new type of organization has gained political power due to their connection to the vigorous defence of conservative and political Islam. So far, they have been intrumentalized by the bigger political parties and oligarchs but their symbolic power is perhaps more significant than their real political power.

As part of this larger trend, Indonesian society has also witnessed more segregation in schooling with state schools being perceived largely for Muslim students. Non-Muslims, especially Christians, are not welcome in some neighbourhoods. There have also been proposals for a sharia-based tourism. Public cemeteries are closed off to non-Muslim dead in certain areas where Christian funerary symbols are deemed offensive and thus banned or vandalized. Religious conservatism also manifests itself in more private and personal spheres, as shown in the phenomenon of "*hijrah*" (a sort of being reborn religiously) among Muslim celebrities where they embrace a pious and sharia-based lifestyle. To a certain degree this has become "the new cool" set against secular Western way of life.

Overall, we see a "conservative turn" in Indonesian Islam, which was made possible by the democratic space that has been opened since the fall of the New Order, as well as by the presence of Middle Eastern influence and networks. This brand of conservative Islamic ideologies is being propagated by various small yet nimbler organizations.[1]

The question is: how deep and real is this phenomenon? Mun'im Sirry is of the opinion that religious intolerance has taken deeper roots in the political and social imaginations of Indonesian Muslims than commonly assumed.[2] This point might be illustrated by intolerant views among various strata of Indonesian Muslim society. Recent studies by Setara Institute and Alvara Institute have found a consistent pattern of conservatism and even radicalism in the educational sector, among school teachers, high school and university students, as well as university professors. There is an alarming situation on college campuses where the religion discourse is dominated by conservative groups with the corresponding lack of rigorous engagement from the mainstream Islamic organization.

II Inclusive Muslim Movement and Theology

The aforementioned development, again, has affected Christian-Muslim relations. It is apparent that the wisdom and skills that naturally come out of the practice of dialogue of life are no longer sufficient to tackle these new and more complex challenges. The practice of dialogue of life itself cannot be taken for granted in certain areas due to the segregation and identity politics mentioned above. Certain areas are closed off to Christians due to the hardening of Islamic identity. Many Christian communities might feel threatened. However, the even tougher challenge is actually faced by the Muslim community itself. The conservative turn above shows an intense internal struggle of self-understanding among Muslims of different strands in dealing with the current situation. This contention has given rise to a stronger movement of inclusive Islam which takes seriously a vision of universal humanism and Indonesian ethical nationalism as a counter-movement to the conservative turn. In terms of Muslim-Christian relations, this inclusive Muslim front is the most promising partner of Christian-Muslim dialogue.

Along this line the programmatic formulation of "Islam Nusantara", or "Archipelagic Islam" (contextualized Islam) by the largest Muslim organization, the Nahdhlatul Ulama (NU), in 2015 is one of the most visible signs of hope for Muslim-Christian relations. In a nutshell, this is a traditional Islam (*al-sunnah wa al-jamaah*) that is practiced, propagated and developed in accordance with the distinctive characteristics of Indonesia's society and culture, including its pluralism and hybridity. In the words of Said Agil Siraj, the current chairman of the Nahdlatul Ulama, "Islam Nusantara" is the newest expression of this hybrid culture. Islam Nusantara is inclusive in character, being founded on the true spirit of religiosity (*ruh al-diniyyah*), which is expressed in lofty character (*aklaqul karimah*), true spirit of patriotism and nationalism (*al-ruh al-wathaniyah*), a spirit of pluralism (*al-ruh al-ta'addudiyyah*), and the spirit of humanism

Albertus Bagus Laksana, S. J.

(*al-ruh al-insaniyyah*).[3]

Surely Indonesian Islam has known figures of dialogue in the past, such as Mr. Abdurrachman Wahid, a Muslim scholar and former chairman of the NU who went on to serve briefly as president of the country (1999-2001), and Dr Nurcholish Madjid, a neo-modernist Muslim thinker whose project was to synthesize Islam and modern ideas of democracy, secularism, pluralism, and gender equality. Largely due to the influence of these thinkers, dialogue with other religions was supported by the main Muslim organizations in the country. This stream of progressive and inclusive Islamic thinking is carried on by the younger generation, such as Zuhairi Misrawi with his inclusive theology of the mercy of God (theology of *basmalah*), Sumanto al-Qurtubi, Mun'im Sirry and Budhy Munawar-Rahman with their critical thought and theology of religious pluralism.[4]

In this regard, it is important to note that around the year 2005, progressive Muslim thinking was actually suffering a blow in both Nahdlatul Ulama and Muhammadiyah, the largest Muslim organizations in the country. These two pillars of inclusive Islam in Indonesia were infiltrated by radical Islamist movements, such as the Hizbut Tahrir and the Tarbiyah with connection to the Muslim Brotherhood, and were thus experiencing a conservative turn as well.[5] Against this background, the formulation of Islam Nusantara cannot be taken for granted. It is a bold and programmatic reformulation of the vision of inclusive Islam that has been practiced in Indonesia. It provides a common framework and platform for this renewed movement of dialogue. It also represents a collective and programmatic statement against rival religious ideology, namely, a narrower framework of Islam that sets itself apart from culture and is marked by iconoclastic and anti-other sentiment. It is also a visionary movement of inclusivity, embracing various forms of "otherness", namely local culture, a common collective identity such as nationalism, and the presence of other religious traditions, all within a very strong emphasis on universal humanism.

It should be emphasized that this programmatic Islam is the fruit of a concerted effort of negotiation. Within this framework, dialogue has become a choice and preference that has to be taken more seriously by the Muslim community because it is part of its self-definition. Since religious contestation has become a new normal in Indonesian pluralistic society, the dialogue of life is no longer enough and the need more creative ways is urgent. This is carried out and done in different ways. Among the most important ones is the construction of Muslim inclusive theologies which are expressed both in public conversations (newspapers etc.) and the academy.

As mentioned, this Muslim inclusive theology is developed in the framework of a shared focus on the common good and ethical nationalism based on humanism. It is also founded on theological humanism, namely, the status of the human person before God, as "spirited creature" who is destined to return to God.[6] Within this framework of the theology of the unity of humankind, Achmad Siddiq (1926-1991), a prominent Muslim theologian of Indonesia, offers a trilogy of brotherhood (*ukhuwah*) with the human brotherhood (*ukhuwwah insaniyyah*) as the crown of the two other forms of brotherhood, namely, the brotherhood of fellow religionists (*ukhuwwah diniyyah*) and brotherhood of fellow citizens (*ukhuwwah wathanniyah*). The words of Ali ibn Abi Thalib are often quoted in support of this vision: "Those who are not your brother or sister in faith are your brother and sister in humanity."[7]

In this religious humanism, the human person is understood as a pilgrim, *homo religiosus et viator*. Religion is understood as a dynamic reality that develops a symbiotic relationship with culture and hybridization with other religions.[8] Amidst high political tension, Helmy Faishal Zaini, the secretary general of the Nahdlatul Ulama proposed a distinctive religio-cultural practice in Indonesian society called *"halal bihalal,"* a collective ritual of reconciliation that is part of the festivity at the end of the month of fasting. The word *"halal bihalal"* means to mutually make right, to forgive each other. Interestingly this word is not found in original Arabic and is not a practice among Arabs. It is a local wisdom that results from a symbiosis between local culture and Islam.

Perhaps the most contextually responsive yet highly controversial aspect of this vision is the reinterpretation of the word *"kafir."* This word is commonly translated as infidel, namely, those who reject God; and in the Indonesian context is often used to refer to non-Muslims, particularly Christians. The NU reasons that this usage is not proper, and prefers to use the word "non-Muslim" to refer to fellow citizens who belong to other religions. Thus, the basis is the idea of equal citizenship (*ukhuwah wathaniyah*) where people are fellow citizens (*muwathinun*). In this regard, the chairman of the NU, Said Aqil Siradj cites the example of the Prophet Muhammad who upon settling in Madina ceased to use the word "*kafir*" to refer to other citizens of Madina who are believers of other religious traditions, and instead used the more neutral word "non-Muslim". And Siradj states further: "In the framework of citizenship, there is no room for labelling others infidel because every citizen has the same status and rights before the Constitution."[10] This point is significant in terms of what it is opposing, namely, the transnational Islam that rejects the validity of nation-states.

This inclusive idea may have been proposed by different Indonesian Muslim theologians in the past, but it is gaining a much stronger and public momentum at present precisely because it is a response to a very urgent challenge in a critical time. For many decades, this kind of inclusivity has been part of the attitude of cultural Islam but it lacked an explicit religious and theological foundation. In this respect, the vision of Islam Nusantara is part of this more conscious effort at self-understanding that has deeper and more serious political and social ramifications.

III Signs of Hope within Christian Communities

With the politicization of Islam and its conservative turn, there are signs that Christian communities across the country are grappling with anxieties, especially in times of political tension. In certain circles and areas, this anxiety or fear is particularly strong. Christian communities feel vulnerable as a minority and (potential) victims of any political upheaval. As a result, the seduction is ever present for them to be concerned with internal affairs and to also play the card of sectarian identity as a minority. However mainstream Churches, namely the Council of Churches in Indonesia (PGI) and the Indonesian Catholic Bishops' Conference (KWI), have renewed their commitment to the common good and ethical nationalism as most recently reflected in their joint Christmas message (2019). Within this framework, they foster ever closer dialogue with their Muslim counterparts.

Within the Catholic Church, the legacy of the first native bishop, Albertus Soegijapranata (1896-1963), has been revived which envisioned Catholic identity as "authentically Catholic and truly Indonesian." Here love of religion and love of nation is combined in ways that are ethical and inclusive, free of chauvinism.[11] Along the same lines, the Theological Commission of the Catholic Bishops' Conference, Protestant institutions and a number of Indonesian theologians have pushed for the development of a contextual theology of inclusive nationalism.

There are many other initiatives at the diocesan level. The Archdiocese of Semarang in Central Java has initiated a movement of "going forth", of facilitating inclusive encounters among citizens and members of Indonesian pluralistic society (in Javanese *"srawung"*) that involves interfaith dialogue. Along this line, Julius Cardinal Darmaatmadja, the cardinal emeritus of Indonesia, has also pushed the Catholic community toward a deeper commitment in the difficult process of nation building. He grounds this involvement in a strong inclusive pneumatological theology of religion, recognizing the work of the Holy Spirit outside the Church, drawing inspiration from *Lumen Gentium* and *Redemptoris Missio*, as well as the theology of prayers of Pope John Paul II (that every authentic prayer is stirred by the Holy Spirit).[12] The Cardinal conceived this theology as a response to the development of inclusive and contextual Muslim theologies from the Nahdlatul Ulama and Muhammadiyah. Along this line, I have tried to develop a contextual Christian-Muslim theology of the name of God as Love and Mercy as a response to the current situation as well as the new development in the Christian theological reflection on mercy by Pope Francis and to the Muslim conception God's name as the Merciful.[13]

IV Conclusion
To foster good and fruitful Christian-Muslim relations is surely a challenge in contemporary Indonesia, but it is not insurmountable. In a special way, one needs to be attentive to political dynamics, but not too overly concerned with it either. For one, the recent politico-religious tensions have shown the resilience of Indonesian society and its commitment to pluralism and dialogue. In general, the direction that Christian-Muslim relations are taking in contemporary Indonesia is in line with the spirit of the Document on Human Fraternity signed by Pope Francis and the Grand Imam of Al-Azhar, Al-Thayeb, in 2019 which focuses on common faith in God that gives birth to human fraternity

geared toward the common good by working together on concrete problems. The framework of Indonesian nation-building seems to be a promising platform for common action between Muslim and Christian communities.

Notes

1. Leonard C. Sebastian and Andar Nubowo, "The 'Conservative Turn' in Indonesian Islam: Implications for the 2019 Presidential Elections," *Asie Visions*, No. 106, March 2019, https://www.ifri.org/en/publications/notes-de-lifri/asie-visions/conservative-turn-indonesian-islam-implications-2019.
2. Mun'im Sirry, "Religious Intolerance in Contemporary Indonesia," in Syafa'atun Almirzanah (ed.), *Kitab Suci dan Para Pembacanya*, Yogyakarta,: UIN Sunan Kaligaja, 2019, 202-203.
3. https://nasional.tempo.co/read/1180695/munas-alim-ulama-nu-sepakati-pengertian-islam-nusantara; see also Akhmad Sahal and Munawir Aziz (eds.), *Islam Nusantara: Dari Ushul Fiqh Hingga Paham Kebangsaan*, Bandung: Mizan Pustaka, 2016.
4. Cf. Zuhairi Misrawi, *Al-Quran Kitab Toleransi: Inklusivisme, Pluralisme dan Multikulturalisme*, Jakarta: Penerbit Fitrah, 2007; Budhy Munawar Rahman, *Islam Pluralis: Wacana Kesetaraan Kaum Beriman*, Paramadina: Srigunting, 2001.
5. Martin van Bruinessen (ed.), Contemporary Developments in Indonesian Islam: Explaining the 'Conservative Turn,' Singapore: Institute of Southeast Asian Studies, 2013, 9.
6. Komaruddin Hidayat, "Peziarah Spiritual," *Kompas* 28 Mei 2019.
7. Quoted in Komaruddin Hidayat, "Peziarah Spiritual," *Kompas* 28 Mei 2019.
8. Komaruddin Hidayat, "Peziarah Spiritual," *Kompas* 28 Mei 2019.
9. Helmy Faishal Zaini, "Halalbihalal Kebangsaan," *Kompas* 4 Juni 2019.
10. https://nasional.tempo.co/read/1180816/said-aqil-di-madinah-nabi-muhammad-tidak-gunakan-istilah-kafir/full&view=ok.
11. On this topic see my essays: "The Pain of Being Hybrid: Catholic Writers and Political Islam in Postcolonial Indonesia," *International Journal of Asian Christianity* 1/2018: 225-249; and "Love of Religion, Love of Nation: Catholic Mission and the Idea of Indonesian Nationalism," *Kritika Kultura* 25 (2015): 91–112.
12. Julius Kardinal Darmaatmadja, *Umat Katolik Dipanggil Membangun NKRI*, Yogyakarta: Kanisius, 2019.
13. Albertus Bagus Laksana, "Naming God Together: Muslim-Christian Theology of Mercy in the Indonesian Context", *Journal of Asian Orientation in Theology* Vol. 1. No. 1 (2019): 1-30.

Academic Collaboration in Germany

KLAUS VON STOSCH

In Germany, Islamic theology is more and more included in the academic programs of public universities. The author tries to show how this development challenges Christian theology and how it reshapes the Muslim community in the country. Moreover, this development opens up new possibilities for Christian-Muslim relations – including some new forms of comparative theology.

Eight years ago German universities started to hire Muslim professors to teach Islamic theology. Today there are eight universities in Germany, funded by the German government, which run programs of Islamic theology. In Germany there is no strict separation between state and religion, but a cooperation where the state tries to support religions as long as they act in accordance with the constitution. This enables the government to fund not only Christian theology – as in the past –, but also Islamic and Jewish theology as is the case now.

This new development is in itself a great sign of hope for Muslim-Christian relations in Germany. It changes the situation of dialogue radically. It becomes possible now to have well trained theologians on both sides who use common methods and share common academic values. Hence, both faith communities are enabled now to attain a new level of mutual understanding. Of course, we need patience and there are also a lot of challenges involved in the establishment of Islamic theology in Germany. But it is an enormous opportunity and gives a lot of hope. Let us focus on this dimension in the article and let us talk of the new horizons which are opened up through this new situation of academic research in German theology.

Klaus Von Stosch

I New Horizons in Exegetical and Historical Work

Islamic theology has always engaged in exegetical and historical work. There is the enormous tradition of *tafsīr* in Islam, and there is also the important tradition of *asbāb an-nuzūl* which tries to identify the reason for the occurrence of certain verses of the Qur'an. Thus, the modern way of doing exegesis can build on a long and powerful tradition within Islam. However, a systematic application of the methods of historical critique has not been practiced yet within Islam. There are several of movements which try first steps in this direction such as for example the Ankara school.[1] But until now a thorough reading of the Qur'an in the light of modern historical research is not part of Islamic theology.

In Germany it is the Corpus Coranicum project in Berlin which has started to read the Qur'an as text of late antiquity and to apply modern methods of philology and historical critique to the understanding of the text.[2] As this research is led by Angelika Neuwirth, it has been done so far in a spirit of appreciation of Islam and its rich intellectual heritage. It can be considered as one of the most important Western movements against the new revisionist tendencies in Western research on Islam. The charisma of Angelika Neuwirth and her great achievements within Arabic and Islamic Studies are a main reason why there is some confidence in historical work on Islam in the Muslim scientific community in Germany. Her project has also close and good connections to research centres in Muslim countries.

One of her students, Zishan Ghaffar, can serve as a great example to illustrate the possibilities for Muslim-Christian relations which can rise from this new development in the academy. Ghaffar studied philosophy, Islamic studies and Protestant theology in Kiel and then received his PhD from one of the new centres of Islamic theology in Germany – in close cooperation with Angelika Neuwirth. Hence he can be seen as one of the first fruits of the new German programs to fund Islamic theology, showcasing which kind of research becomes possible through such funding and cooperation.

His PhD has been published in 2018 with the title *The historical Muhammad in Islamic theology. On methods and criteria of the research of the life of Muhammad.*[3] The thesis has the ambitious goal of comparing Western research on Muhammad with Western research on Jesus and it shows that the methodological innovations of the third quest which have been so successful in Western research on Jesus have not been applied fully to the research on Muhammad. Thus, as Ghaffar shows convincingly, it is the deficiency in Western research that is the reason for the purely revisionist tendencies in some Western schools of research. Hence, if some revisionists argue that Muhammad has probably never lived – an idea which was famously defended by the first Muslim professor of Islamic theology in Münster, Muhammad Sven Kalisch – Ghaffar's response is that these kinds of results are only possible because these scholars (such as Kalisch or the school of Saarbrücken) are simply not up to date in their methods of research. Hence, for Ghaffar, the antidote against the Western and modern critique of Islam is not a Muslim withdrawal from modern methods of research, but a more accurate way of using these methods. Ghaffar invites Muslims to do their job simply more accurately than their Western colleagues and to beat them with their own weapons: scrutiny, scholarship and historical criticism.

This more apologetic motive of Ghaffar does not mean that he is apologetic against Judaism and Christianity. He learned from Angelika Neuwirth that the Qur'an can only be understood together with its intertextual relations. And these relations force Muslims not only to read the Bible, but also to learn Syriac and to read the church fathers and rabbinic intertexts. Hence Ghaffar's research is highly dependent on a close cooperation with Christian and Jewish theologians. When one of my PhD students asked Ghaffar whether he thinks that a Muslim comparative theology is possible, he simply responded that this is the only way to do Islamic theology. If it is not comparative, it is not able to understand the Qur'an. At the same time, he is self-confident enough to challenge not only Western research but also Christian theology with the results of his research.

Even more exciting than his thesis is Ghaffar's second book that has just been published with the title *The Qur'an in its historical context. Eschatological and Apocalyptical motives in the middle-Meccan Surahs*.[4] It makes Ghaffar visible as a mature scholar who reads the Qur'an together with the intertexts from Christianity and Judaism in the light of late antique history. Similar to Western scholars such as Sidney Shoemaker[5] he is aware of the apocalyptical and messianic motives of the

Qur'an. In meticulous philological work he identifies the Christian and Jewish interlocutors of the Qur'an and – pace Shoemaker – shows how the Qur'an criticizes any kind of apocalyptical discourse because it was used by the theology of the Byzantine Empire of his time. This makes the Qur'an visible as an anti-apocalytical, anti-messianic and anti-imperial text which tries to set theology free from political demands. Of course, this kind of analysis cannot simply be repeated for the Medinan time. But it is already outstanding to show this kind of tendency for the Meccan period of the Qur'an and it is literally speaking ground-breaking research on the Qur'an.

Especially in our time, where some politicians in the West try to develop Christian apocalyptic messages again, it can be instructive not only for Muslims to see how the Qur'an reacts to this kind of political agenda. In sum, the Qur'an reacts with powerful theological arguments – entirely peaceful and without any violence. If this kind of analysis becomes more widespread among our Muslim colleagues, it will be a very helpful sign of hope against modern prophets announcing the clash of civilizations and the decline of the Christian West.

II New Horizons in Systematic and Philosophical Work

The situation of Christian theology in Germany is a very special one. Protestant and Catholic theology have both been profoundly influenced by enlightenment thinking and German idealism. In some sense, not Aquinas or Luther but Kant and Hegel are the most influential German church fathers. This is challenging for the churches in Germany, but at the same time helpful and productive for the participation of Christianity in intellectual life in the country. Both Protestants and Catholics have created a special German form of free will theism which shapes public debates, and which has influenced religious communities as well. To be sure, there are some more conservative colleagues who do not think that this development has been particularly helpful. And there are also some postmodern and post-liberal theologians who would like to change the style of German theology. But still the heritage of transcendental criticism and free will theology is very influential within German Christianity.

For Islamic systematic theology, this challenge can become very productive and promises to provoke a lot of new forms of thinking among

Muslims. We can see how scholars likes Ahmad Milad Karimi try to use Hegel and Heidegger to reconstruct *kalām* in a very productive and highly original way.[6] And scholars like Mouhanad Khorchide become influential with their ideas of using free will theology to renew Islam as the religion of mercy.[7] It is true that this development has received considerable criticism. But even a scholar as Muna Tatari who defends the centrality of justice as decisive category of Islam against too much Christianizing talk of mercy, establishes her ideas within the framework of transcendental philosophy and with the help of insights of Kant.[8] Hence there is already an ongoing debate on the use of free will philosophy within the Muslim academic community, and the question is not so much whether it can be accepted, but in which way it is to be used. This helps Muslims in Germany to participate productively in the intellectual development of the country, and it makes sense that one of the most important public intellectuals in Germany nowadays is a Muslim: Navid Kermani – a very influential thinker in politics, literature and theology.[9]

However, there are also important tendencies which are critical of too much systematic innovation within Islam. Some scholars prefer going back to their medieval sources and developing some Aristotelian or Neo-Platonic types of *kalām*. But the interesting point is that all scholars try to find coalitions with Christians and Jews in their way of doing theology. Although there was some suspicion of theology as a Christian project in the beginning, today most Muslim intellectuals welcome the development of systematic Islamic theology and they understand it as a form of thinking which helps Muslims to interface as equals within society and with Christian theologians.

For Christian theology this development is challenging and fruitful at the same time. When Karimi develops a Hegelian theology without Trinitarian framework or when Kermani uses Jewish writers and philosophers to reshape the Muslim role in German society, this creates new ideas and needs for rethinking Christianity and its role for our society. Thus, the new power of Islamic theology in Germany challenges also Christians to become more confident in their own theological role. And it enables a new form of comparative theology.

Klaus Von Stosch

III New Horizons through Comparative, Dialogical and Interactive Theology

The development of Islamic theology in Germany is a sign of hope not only for Western societies, but also for Muslim-Christian relations. It also enables a new form of comparative theology which is very much performed as collaborative, dialogical and interactive theology. Islamic theologies are always developed in close relation to Christian theologies. Sometimes the Christian theologians do not really know what to do with those new colleagues, especially because most of them have never tried to be responsive to Islam in their academic work. But more and more younger theologians are developing interest in comparative work. Usually comparative theology needs considerable expertise in at least two religions. Today in Germany the close cooperation between Christians, Muslims and Jews at the new theological centres in the German academia make it possible to develop comparative theology as a collaborative project. Up to now only the university of Paderborn follows this way programmatically. But more and more other universities are becoming aware of the rich possibilities of research which can shape German theology. As theology is organized in different confessional faculties and institutes in Germany, this development does not simply lead to interreligious theology, but to co-operations, dialogue and interactions. I would like to summarize all these kinds of theologies under the umbrella category of comparative theology. And it is a sign of hope that many younger scholars from many nations use the German academic context to contribute to this emerging field of research.

Let me conclude with an example from one of my Iranian PhD students who develops his own Shiite theology in this kind of collaborative, dialogical and interactive atmosphere. He is part of my current research project on Mary in the Qur'an which brings together scholars from different religions and confessions for a better understanding of Mary in the Muslim tradition. After our last meeting which was very much an intertextual reading of some parts of Surah Maryam with some verses from Syriac church fathers, he said: "Well, when reading the Qur'an in the light of those Christian debates and when listening to all those Christians responding to these verses, I get the feeling that this part of the Qur'an is not for me – at least not for me alone." He understood that God's word is not a word for a certain tribe or nation and that we can never own it. We have to learn how it challenges all of us. And in cooperation beyond the borders of our religions and denominations we can become responsive in our different theologies also to those prophetic voices which we have ignored so far. For me this is a great sign of hope for all of us.

Notes

1. Felix Körner, *Revisionist Koran Hermeneutics in Contemporary Turkish University Theology*, Würzburg: Ergon, 2005.
2. Angelika Neuwirth, *Der Koran als Text der Spätantike. Ein europäischer Zugang*, Berlin: Verlag der Weltreligionen, 2010.
3. Zishan Ghaffar, *Der historische Muhammad in der islamischen Theologie. Zur Kriterienfrage in der Leben-Muhammad-Forschung*, Paderborn: Ferdinand Schöningh/ Brill Deutschland 2018.
4. Zishan Ghaffar, *Der Koran in seinem religions- und weltgeschichtlichen Kontext. Eschatologie und Apokalyptik in den mittelmekkanischen Suren*, Paderborn: Ferdinand Schöningh/ Brill Deutschland 2020.
5. Sidney Shoemaker, *The Apocalypse of Empire. Imperial Eschatology in Late Antiquity and Early Islam*, Philadelphia: University of Pennsylvania Press, 2018.
6. Milad Karimi, *Hingabe. Grundfragen der systematisch-islamischen Theologie*, Freiburg-Berlin-Wien 22015.
7. Mouhanad Khorchide, *Islam ist Barmherzigkeit. Konturen einer modernen Religion*, Freiburg-Basel-Wien: Herder 22016.
8. Muna Tatari, *Gott und Mensch im Spannungsverhältnis von Gerechtigkeit und Barmherzigkeit. Versuch einer islamisch begründeten Positionsbestimmung*, Münster: Waxmann 2016.
9. Michael Hofmann/ Klaus von Stosch/ Swen Schulte Eickholt, *Navid Kermani*, Würzburg: Königshausen & Neumann, 2019.

The Dialogue School in Belgium

LAURIE JOHNSTON

Beyond high-level meetings of clerics or scholars, where today does genuine Muslim-Christian dialogue take place? Despite tensions and prejudices in Belgian society, there are also spaces where ordinary Muslims and Catholics are able to meet and speak about faith in a significant way. Often, Catholic schools are providing these spaces. Prompted by the growing numbers of Muslim students in their midst, Catholic schools and universities in Belgium have responded by re-examining their mission and adopting new modes of religious education – notably, the dialogue-school model in Flanders. While such changes are challenging and have often provoked backlash, they could lead to a more authentic understanding of Catholic identity and mission in a diverse society.

In the past decade or so, there has been a change in how Belgians speak about minorities in their society. While in the past most Belgians would have referred to 'Turks' or 'Moroccans' (two of the largest immigrant groups in the country), now there is a tendency to refer to these groups collectively, as 'Muslims'. This new focus on religious, rather than ethnic or national identity, emerges partly from the growth of the 'Clash of Civilizations' trope – a trope which gained power after the terrorist attacks of September 11, 2001 in the US. Later, the 2015 Paris attacks, in which a number of Belgian nationals were implicated, and the 2016 bombings at the Brussels airport and subway increased many Belgians' sense that they have a 'Muslim problem.'

This collective reference to 'Muslims' is problematic; it can be a means of 'othering' and marginalizing groups that remain disadvantaged in Belgian society. References to Islam are often used as a cudgel by nationalist politicians who assert the incompatibility of Islam with Belgian culture. In addition, referring to Turks and Moroccans collectively is rather odd, given that those two groups do not necessarily perceive themselves as having a great deal in common, given their cultural, linguistic, and theological differences.

At the same time, this growing discussion about Islam in Belgian society also presents important opportunities for dialogue. Lieven Boeve, a theologian and the Director General of the Flemish Secretary for Catholic Education, has written about the way that attention to Islam is creating space for greater discussion of religion. He says, "Islam is reminding westerners that there is something called religion. Secularization came first, now we're confronted by pluralization. Pluralization can feed secularization, but also it interrupts secularization."[1] As an example of this, he and others have noted that growing awareness about Ramadan has also prompted many in Belgium to become more curious about Lent. In a way, the Catholic Church in Belgium is indebted to Muslims for pushing back against secularization and revealing the impossibility of a 'neutral' public space that is free from religious identities. Of course, not all Catholics see things this way, and as Boeve also points out, pluralization presents many challenges of its own. Often, he says, the reappearance of religion in the public sphere takes place "in a polarizing way."[2] In a country that is perhaps best described as post-Catholic, there are conflicting opinions about what role religion ought to play in society.

Nevertheless, for many Catholics in Belgium, now is an opportunity to re-examine their faith, vocation, and institutional identities – and this re-examination is often taking place through dialogue with Muslims. A key site for this dialogue is the Catholic school system, which plays a major role in Belgium. Nearly 70% of all children attend Catholic schools – even though practicing Catholics are few, and weekly attendance at mass is in the single digits in the overall population. Many parents choose Catholic schools for their children because of their reputation for educational quality. Some Muslim parents opt for Catholic schooling because they believe that their religious faith may be more welcomed and supported at a Catholic school than at a state school. As one school director in Belgium told me, these parents think that "It's better for my child to be in a place where God is respected."[3] It is somewhat surprising to see Muslim parents choosing a Catholic school over a state school because in state schools, students are entitled to education in their own religions – Muslims can attend classes on Islam, Catholics on Catholicism, etc. However, the majority of students in state schools attend an alternative course that is known as 'Non-confessional ethics.' Some Muslim families do choose state schools so that their children can attend classes on Islam, though often they have mixed feelings about the quality of these classes. But overall, a significant proportion of Muslim children in Belgium attend Catholic schools. Because Muslim populations in Belgium tend to be concentrated in certain geographic areas (notably Brussels and other urban centres), Catholic schools in these areas sometimes have student populations that are entirely Muslims of Turkish descent, or entirely Muslims of Moroccan descent.

What does it mean for a school to be Catholic when the majority – or even the entirety - of the students are Muslim? And how should classes in Catholic theology be taught to Muslim students? These questions are not unique to Belgium. But it is indeed remarkable to see how Catholic theologians and school administrators there have embraced these theological and practical challenges. This is one of the signs of hope in Belgium today: religion classes in Catholic schools have, in many cases, become important spaces of interreligious dialogue. Unlike the state schools, which segregate students for religion classes, students in Catholic schools all attend religion courses together. Thus, these classes provide some of the only spaces in Belgian society where Muslims, Catholics, and others have the opportunity to engage in serious dialogue about matters of faith. Those who design the curriculum have seized the opportunity that this offers. On both the Flemish-speaking and French-speaking sides of Belgium, courses in religion explicitly invite students to a dialogue about meaning, belief, and faith.

In Flanders, the Catholic school system adopted a new religious education curriculum in 2014 called the Catholic Dialogue School. One of the architects of the curriculum has described their efforts:

How can religious education prepare pupils for a culturally and religiously diverse society and still hold on its denominational (especially Christian) identity? In the hermeneutic-communicative model of religious education, difference itself becomes the matter, not just because of external circumstances, such as a growing multicultural and multi-religious context, but in the name of the identity of Christian education itself. In this approach, the tension between difference and identity is made the locus of religious education. Standing in this tension is preparing the next generations for life and is also the place where…God reveals himself. Teachers training should first and foremost help future teachers to deal with this tension and to mobilize it as the engine of the communicative religious learning process.[4]

The curriculum ultimately aims to help students move towards what Paul Ricoeur called "post-critical belief." While some efforts to teach religious education in diverse communities have emphasized 'values education', this curriculum is notable for its emphasis on sharing the specifics of beliefs and stories – but in a mode that is dialogical and open. One young Muslim student explained this powerfully:

Stories are important to teach children something…they contribute to the formation of identity. At least that was the case for me. At home I got to hear the Islamic stories, at school the Christian. This turned out to be an important added value for my personal development. Both sides of the story made me the practicing Muslim I am today. That is why I am not in favour of a broad 'philosophy of life' at school. It lacks stories that reinforce identity.[5]

Despite positive responses from many students like this young man, the adoption of this new curriculum has produced a backlash from some prominent Catholics. Some argue that Catholic schools should be 'monological' and tell only the Catholic story. To them, allowing the Islamic story to be told in a Catholic schools is a compromise of identity. But ironically, attending school with Muslims and hearing about their stories may be the best way to slow the rapid loss of Catholic identity among young Belgians. Data from Xaveriuscollege, a Jesuit high school in Antwerp with significant number of Muslim students, bears this out.

In survey data, it is clear that the Muslim students at Xaveriuscollege, by the time they graduate, overwhelmingly describe their own beliefs as falling into the 'post-critical believing' category – a key goal of the Dialogue School curriculum.[6] But for the 'white' students, there is a similar pattern as at many other Catholic schools in Belgium – dramatically declining levels of religious belief and Catholic affiliation during high school. By graduation, most of these students have become secular relativists with few personal convictions at all. A small number also describe themselves as hostile to religion of any kind. But while this overall pattern holds at Xaveriuscollege, this decline is less severe. As one researcher puts it, "Despite - or thanks to (?) – the Muslim population in Xaveriuscollege, there are relatively more post-critical believers among the non-Muslim students there, compared to the Flemish average." In addition, the non-Muslim students have a lower rate of hostility to religion altogether.[7] While it is still true that the school is swimming against an overwhelming tide of disaffiliation from Catholicism, it seems that the Muslim students are helping the school to push back a bit.

This finding is significant partly because so many Catholic school leaders express a great deal of anxiety about having many Muslim students attend their schools. One theology teacher told me that her school cannot permit Muslim girls to wear the veil because then more Muslims will want to attend, and their school will come be known as a 'Muslim school' and perhaps even one of *les écoles poubelles* [garbage schools].[8] Clearly there is significant class and racial anxiety at play, and not merely a religious issue. Some directors perceive any accommodations for Muslim students as a slippery slope away from both Catholic identity and educational quality.

The question of Catholic identity in relation to Islam becomes particularly fraught at schools where Catholic identity itself is rather impoverished. One teacher noted grimly that at her school some teachers only refer to the school's Catholic identity when they are disciplining disorderly students in the hallway: "You can't behave that way! This is a CATHOLIC school."[9] In some contexts, the term Catholic is virtually a synonym for 'civilized' or 'normal' – clearly a usage that marginalizes others.

Nevertheless, some Catholic leaders are responding to the presence of Muslims by deepening their own understanding of Catholic identity and mission. Indeed, in some cases Catholics are articulating their vocation as one that particularly involves Muslims. Sometimes this is implicit: a teacher at an all-Muslim Catholic school said simply, "When it comes to Catholic identity, the most important thing is to *live* Christianly, to respond to children who are in need."[10] One school director put it even more explicitly, however:

The message of the Gospel is to attend to the marginalized in society. The 'option for the poor' means that to be Catholic, we should pay attention to the needs of Muslims first because they are marginalized in Belgium.[11]

Even the architects of the Catholic Dialogue School curriculum acknowledge that since it appears to be too late to stem the decline of Catholicism among young people in Belgium, the most important mission of the Catholic Dialogue School may actually be to help create a well-educated, 'enlightened' Islam.[12]

More broadly, the situation in Belgium offers an opportunity to ask what duties Catholics have towards the faith of Muslims. Beyond theological dialogues about the Abrahamic God, how ought we relate to one another's spiritual practices in day to day life? Particularly in a situation where Catholics enjoy significant institutional power, what might it mean for these institutions to live out *Ex Corde Ecclesiae's* admonition that "A Catholic University is to promote the pastoral care of all members of the university community?"[13] With that admonition in mind, I asked several directors of Catholic schools in Belgium, "Do you think it is a good thing for your Muslim students to pray? To fast?" This question was an attempt to elicit their theological assumptions about the nature of prayer, the purpose of fasting, the nature of Muslims' faith in God, etc. In several cases, it was clear that my interview subjects were quite uncomfortable with this question. One director quickly answered, "It is none of my business."[14] Another director, however, said that this was wrong: "We believe in the *cura personalis*," he noted. And he went on to say, "When no one in the world prays, it is a disaster for the world."[15] Indeed it is a disaster for the world when no one prays. And it is sometimes Muslims in Belgium who are reminding Catholics of this. This reminder may not always be comfortable, though; one school director described Muslims as holding up a mirror to Catholics in Belgium today. In a mirror, "I may see things about myself that I do not want to see."[16]

There are many factors that pose challenges for Muslim-Catholic dialogue in Belgium today: political debates about the role of Islam in Belgian society, polarized opinions about religion and national identity, young Belgian Muslims leaving to join ISIS, migration, populism. Yet, at the level of the day-to-day problems of living together, genuine dialogue takes place. For instance, the question of whether Muslim girls are allowed to wear hijab to school is a neuralgic one in Belgium – but it is also an opening to conversation. The Catholic school administration in Flanders has, in fact, a staff member whose full time job is to visit Catholic schools in Flanders and facilitate conversations about their veil policies. In a sense, his job is entirely devoted to helping Catholic schools examine their attitudes about the role of Muslims at Catholic school, and therefore, the role of Muslims in Belgian society as a whole. Instead of shrill conversations in the media, these schools are engaging in genuine dialogue – about, but also *with* their Muslim students. To the extent that they are willing to embrace it, Catholics have an important mediating role to play in Belgian society, particularly by providing a space for dialogue in the schools. And if they are willing to embrace it, Muslims too have an important role to play in inviting Catholics to live out their mission and identity in more authentic ways. Together, their dialogue can help build bridges across the many fractures in Belgian society.

Notes

1. Interview with Lieven Boeve, Brussels, 20 March 2018.
2. Ibid.
3. Interview B, with a teacher of theology, Brussels, 19 April 2018. (Most interview subjects are identified only by a letter in order to preserve the confidentiality of the interviewee and their school.)
4. Didier Pollefeyt, 'Difference Matters: A Hermeneutic-Communicative Concept of Didactics of Religion in a European Multi-Religious Context.' *Journal of Religion Education* 56.1(2008), 9-17.
5. Bertrand Goethals and Jozefien Van Huffel. 'Dossier. Als je op school je eigen geloof verkent vanuit een ander standpunt.' Kerk & leven, *jaargang* 80 nr. 29-30-31 (2019), 10-11.
6. Didier Pollefeyt & Jan Bouwens, *Enhancing Catholic School Identity (ECSI) project*, Katholieke Universiteit Leuven, Belgium. Research 'Theologie, Religie en Onderwijs' in Xaveriuscollege, Borgerhout, 2011-2012.
7. Ibid.
8. Interview H, with a teacher of theology, Brussels, 26 March 2018.
9. Interview B, with a teacher of theology, Brussels, 19 April 2018
10. Ibid.
11. Interview G, with a school director, Flanders, 26 April 2018.
12. Interview with Didier Pollefeyt and Jan Bouwens, Leuven, 16 February 2018.
13. *Ex Corde Ecclesiae*, Art. 6.
14. Interview I, with a school director, Wallonia, 8 February 2018.
15. Interview J, with a school director, Flanders, 5 June 2018.
16. Interview E., with a former school director, Brussels, 26 April 2018.

Grassroots Initiatives in Turkey

CLAUDIO MONGE, O.P.

Interreligious dialogue in Turkey since the 1980s has experienced a curious and sometimes almost schizophrenic interchange between original initiatives and, sometimes, even unique in their kind, periods of of major impasse due to the vicissitudes of political life, which often and deliberately conditioned and guided interreligious relations by manipulating them. Following the failed coup d'etat in 2016, the banishment of members of the Islamic Hizmet *(service) movement, which from the 70s encourgaed 80% of the initiatives and platforms of interreligious dialogue in Turkish territory and elsewhere, inflicted a blow to the heart of the more institutional dimension of interreligious dialogue, but encouraged the development of initiatives perhaps less spectacular but more widespread.*

On 25 April 2002 the Holy See signed a Declaration of Intentions with the President of the Turkish Religious Affairs Office (*Diyanet*) to promote interreligious dialogue.[1] The Catholic news agency *Zenit* described this initiative, which in the Christian world seems somewhat strange, as without precedent, but in reality it is not something unusual given the special nature of relations between the religious and government authorities in nations with a Muslim tradition. In the absence in the Islamic world of a central religious authority and a recognised hierarchy there is something of an obligation to begin dialogue with the various governments.

For decades, however, it was a dialogue too closely linked to the vicissitudes of political life, which often and willingly conditions or steers interreligious relations by manipulating them, sometimes unfairly attributing to them hidden and secret aims: the well-known tendency to fabricate "conspiracy" theories, well-rooted in the culture of the countries in the South of the Mediterranean. In the 80s and 90s the dialogue initiatives were also closely linked to prominent charismatic figures and their personal initaitives: the Latin Apostolic Vicar of Istanbul, Mgr. Dubois (former collaborator of Mgr. Roncalli, Apostolic Legate in Turkey at the time of the Second World War) and the Greek-Orthodox Patriarch Bartolomew (enthroned in the Phanar 1991) above all. However, those years also saw the start of inter-university collaboration, such as that between the University of Ankara and Rome's Pontifical Gregorian University (1986) aimed at increasing mutual knowledge between the Islamic and Christian worlds (highlighting their very diversity and internal complexity) and encouraging the concrete exchange of students, and also academic personnel for shared teaching and research projects. Right up to our time this official agreement has encouraged the development of an intense network of more informal exchanges: visits, partnerships, didactic mentoring. Turkey, crossroads of history and holy land of religions, attracts internal symposia and conferences (Myra, Harran, Antioch, Urfa, Mardin, Konya, Ephesus, Tarsus, Istanbul), where there is an attempt to develop new ways of collaboration for dialogue and fraternity among the children of Abarham (an explicit reference to the believers in the great Monotheistic Faiths).

The bilateral relations between the Holy See and the Diyanet continued in those years. In September 2012, the secretary of the Pontifical Council for Interreligious Dialogue, Fr Miguel Ángel Ayuso Guixot, meeting in Turkey the President of the Diyanet, Dr. Mehmet Görmez, shared the idea of re-launching the old agreement of 2002. So in May 2013, Fr Ayuso and Mgr. Akasheh, head of the section for Islam in the Pontifical Council for Interreligious Dialogue, went to Turkey to pay a courtesy visit to the President of the Diyanet, to define the terms of formal collaboration between the two bodies.[2] These contacts demonstrate a certain mutual goodwill, but were never followed by substantial changes in the rather formal and general relationships. In fact, there is even the risk of sometimes transforming interreligious dialogue into a somewhat spectacular event with an end itself, increasingly distant from daily experience, in a country where, especially in the urban centres, cultural and religious diversity are increasing exponentially, nourished by the significant impact of migration, consequence of the regional bloody conflicts (Afghanistan, Kuwait, Iraq, up to the most recent Syrian crisis), without forgetting the constant migrations from the Far East (in particular Filipinos and Koreans)

In fact, interreligious dialogue and equidistance are not always at the centre of the Turkish political agenda. In September 2013 Turkey's new phase under the presidency of Tayip Erdogan opened with school reforms. In particular, Koranic religious teaching and education was extended to all types of schools, of every level and character. Up to that moment it had been limited solely to the Imam Hatip Lisesi, to the religious schools aimed at forming future teachers of religion and employees of the Diyanet; these could be accessed only after the completion of the eight years of compulsory schooling (the reform makes access possible from primary school). The concrete fear is that of an increase in discrimination of non-Mulsim students or of those Muslims belonging to minority groups within Islam which ask not to use the religious teaching of the Sunni Hanafi group. Another significant new element of the reform in question is that the graduates of the religious schools, contrary to what has happened up to now, can have access to all the university faculties which entitle you to the key posts in public administration.

The second half of the first decade of the third millennium has been characterised by a worrying focus of lethal attacks inflicted on Christian subjects of different denominations, which filled international media news reports, too: Fr Andrea Santoro, the Catholic priest killed in 2006; two native Turkish Protestants, Necati Aydin and Ugur Yuksel, and the German Tilmann Geske, killed in Malatya in 2007. Then, in July 2009, the German Catholic businessman, Gregor Kerkeling, was killed by a young madman while he was walking with his Turkish fiancée, apparently due to his Christian faith. Finally, we remember the tragic murder of Mgr Luigi Padovese, Apostolic Vicar of Anatolia, killed on 3 June 2010 by his driver, Murat Altun. Among the causes of this violence is an extremism fruit of major disinformation associated with a slander spread by certain organs of information to the detriment of Christians. There is also a certain more or less explicit intolerance encouraged within the sphere of educational programmes.

The simple association of the Christian presence with not well-defined neo-crusade programmes or the total ignorance of the complex diversity between historical Christian churches and Christian sectarian neo-movements encourage a multiplication of initiatives of encounter focussed on mutual knowledge and respect, on the part of both Christian and Muslim working groups which take on the task of opening new and alternative pathways, compared to a generic common sense. The Islamic-Christian symposia held at Yeşilköy, part of Istanbul, between 2003-2008, convoked initially by the Cappuchin Friars of the Custody of the Holy Land and then continued between 2010-2014 as a Franciscan Inter-congregational project, in collaboration with the Dominicans and the Jesuits, had the aim of highlighting a reflection which never loses sight of the lived experience, at the heart of a society seen as a network of relationships of inclusive citizenship (an anticipation of the themes which would be re-launched in February 2019 by the famous *Document on Human Fraternity for World Peace*, signed in Abu Dhabi).

This insight, which became particularly urgent in July 2016, the year of the failed coup d'etat against President Erdoğan, when an extremely delicate and tense phase was opened in a dramatically polarised Turkish society. But it was also a blow to the heart inflicted on the institutional and representational dimension of interreligious dialogue, in that it marked the start of a state war with no boundaries against the members of the Islamic movement *Hizmet* (service) and its leader Fethullah Gülen, of which, originally, the founder of the AKP party was a creation. From the end of the 70s, Hizmet encouraged 80% of the initiatives and platforms of Turkish interreligious dialogue, both within the country and abroad, with offices in the majority of European, North American and Asian cities and a widespread network of Islamic teaching centres on the four continents. His banishment meant there was a significant decline in "official" interreligious dialogue, at a high institutional level. Now, at a distance of some years from this "earthquake", initiatives are beginning to flourish again, certainly more discreet and local but, sometimes, also more profound and longing not to be simply random events: initiatives in the sense of a greater listening, of a mutual knowledge and, also, of a comparative study of the different religious traditions, in relation to the existential needs at the heart of complex and multi-religious societies.

The need to re-build patiently an atmosphere of trust and mutual respect, in a context characterised, instead, by suspicion and the negative encouragement in informing about the hypothetical enemy, highlights new methodological demands in the practice of true interreligious dialogue, and particularly Islamic-Christian. The meetings promoted by the DoSt-I (Dominican Study – Istanbul), the cultural centre run by the Dominican Fathers right in Istanbul's historic centre, since 2004 have tried to implement above all a seminar-style *modus operandi*; they are aimed at small groups whose participants have a very homogeneous preparation and to a certain level and have already developed a mutual knowledge, so as to be able to offer a really shared contribution to the work of research, study and the reading of texts, while at the same time being encouraged not to ignore the existential dimension of their profession of faith. The area of interaction is not limited to theology, but extends to history, archaeology, philosophy, and into art and architecture.

The power of gestures (such as attention and presence at the major faith points of each tradition), the discovery of common symbols (such as water symbol of purification or fire, referring back to transcendent inspiration) and those proper to our respective traditions, in a narrative in which the *terms* to be used are carefully chosen so that they can be in some way signficative in the cultural horizon of the other. Finally, the sharing of *spaces*. The Turkish tradition of welcome has always encouraged a very natural access to the places of worship of the different faiths and down the years the care for welcome has been improved by developing a pedagogy of the narrative, and this in a Christian, Catholic context in particular (given the architectural importance of its historical places of worship), as well as in the Muslim context, in the great historical city mosques, which are also important tourist attractions (not for nothing has the Diyanet, in recent years, organised a service of religious welcome, to illustrate the pillars of Islam, generally with the help of young university students, able to express themselves at least in English).

With regard to the power of gestures and the sharing of spaces here it is impossible not to call to mind the importance especially of the last two papal visits to Turkey: Benedict XVI in 2006 and Francis in 2014. The reflection of the two Popes in the Sultan Ahmet mosque in Istanbul (better known as the Blue Mosque) represents more than just a publicity stunt. Benedict XVI, who had never hidden his reticence about following his predecessor on the "Assisi path" stating, on the occasion of the twentieth anniversary of the Historic Interreligious Prayer,[3] that, even when people are gathered together to pray for peace, prayer must be undertaken in accordance with the distinctive paths of the different religions, by entering the best known mosque in Istanbul, seemed in the silence to leave room for a more spiritual, almost intimistic approach. In Turkey, the profound distance which had been created between Assisi and Regensburg,[4] seemed to be reduced anew. If the intervention on German territory seemed, to the most attentive observers, more than a simple error of communication, this symbolic change in Turkish territory (which some courageously defined as a true and proper "conversion") cannot be reduced even to a simple media operation. To go barefoot beyond the entrance threshold of the Islamic place of worship not to stake a claim but to put oneself in harmony with a spiritual atmosphere which refers to a beyond, to a God who summons humanity beyond the strategies and games of influence which more often drive the intentions of governments and religious leaders, represented a highly significant change in mindset (and more in continuity with certain gestures of John Paul II). In 2014, Pope Francis, with the frankness which characterises him, would definitively close the unpleasant debate on the theme: "Can a pope pray in an Islamic place of worship?", by openly acknowledging, in the course of the return flight from Istanbul to Rome, that he had prayed in the Blue Mosque, urged by the Grand Mufti to unite himself with the verses of Surah 19 of the Koran about the Virgin Mary.

Today, those unique events have become a practice of daily life, as when students of the Imam Hatip (Turkish religious schools, where there is separation between males and females) prepare for visits to the church attached to the DoSt-I, for once leaving the exclusively Islamic horizon of their daily studies, seeking to listen and become filled with a symbolic horizon very different from the one which they are accustomed to facing (suffice to think of the iconic dimension of Christian art, compared to the total Islamic aniconism).

This is the indispensable and symbolic premise of the entry into the common space also comprising shared values, for the construction of a living side-by-side in civil community. The real challenge is still the ability to put forward a "lived faith", even before it is confessed and celebrated, to know how to give a specific weight too to the lived experience of the one who believes differently but sincerely and in a coherent manner.

Translated by Patricia Kelly

Notes

1. The Declaration was co-signed by the President of the Pontifical Council for Interreligious Dialogue, Cardinal Arinze, and by the President of the Diyanet, Mehmet Nuri Yilmaz (cfr. Pisai, *Islamochristiana*, Rome, 28 /2002, p. 234).
2. Cfr. Redazione, "Papa e Santa Sede", *Zenit*, May 08/2014, fonte internet: https://it.zenit.org/articles/a-roma-dialogo-interreligioso-tra-santa-sede-e-turchia-2/.
3. Benedict XVI, Letter to the Bishop of Assisi-Nocera Umbra-Gualdo Tadino on the occasion of the 20th anniversary of the Interreligious Meeting of Prayer for Peace (2 September 2006): http://www.vatican.va/content/benedict-xvi/en/letters/2006/documents/hf_ben-xvi_let_20060902_xx-incontro-assisi.html
4. Regensburg is the university where Pope Benedict XVI gave his famous lecture on 12 September 2006 on the theme *Faith, Reason and the University*, in the course of which, wanting to introduce the crucial idea that to act irrationally is contrary to God's nature, the speaker made reference to the stance taken by a Byzantine emperor at war with the Turks and scornful towards the message of Mohammed. The choice led to months of indignant and sometimes violent worldwide Islamic reaction.

Collaboration for Peace in Nigeria

MARINUS CHIJIOKE IWUCHUKWU

After decades of Muslim-Christian conflicts, there are today growing numbers of Muslim-Christian collaborations that advocate for peaceful coexistence of Muslims and Christians in Nigeria. This article will examine a number of these new organizations as well as similar organizations either set up by the government or serving as NGOs in different parts of Nigeria to ameliorate or end incidents of Muslim-Christian violent conflicts. How have these organizations and the growing phenomenon of advocating and promoting healthy Christian-Muslim relations addressed existing bias and antagonism between Christians and Muslims? And what ways can more dividends of healthy Muslim-Christian relations be harnessed and promoted? These are some of the questions that this article seeks to address.

After the Independence of Nigeria in 1960, the political tension and conflict among the different ethnic components of Nigeria (especially between the south-east and the north) spiralled into a civil war (1967-1970) and an attempt to secede from the nation by the south-east. At the end of the civil war there were some concerted efforts to douse or even eliminate existing ethnic rivalries. However, the marked religious differences between the different ethnicities served as outlet for continued tension, rivalry, and conflict. While most members from the dominant Hausa-Fulani of northern Nigeria consider themselves Muslims by default, most of the ethnicities in the south identify as Christians. The minority ethnicities of the middle belt and northern Nigeria are in some estimations evenly split into Christianity and Islam. Therefore, the old north-south political divide and rivalry used religion to further enunciate their differences. A growing

Christian-Muslim rivalry snowballed into violent conflicts starting in 1978 on the pretext of Sharia implementation and its constitutionality. The epicentres of such violence have been for the most part several cities in the north and middle belt, and virtually every major city in northern Nigeria has scars of such devasting religious motivated violence.

With the birth of Boko Haram around 2002 and the rise of its militancy from 2009, religiously motivated conflict in northern Nigeria took a different turn and tone. This is because the Boko Haram militants viciously attacked both Muslims and Christians as well as public establishments. As a fundamentalist and militaristic faction of Islam, it was vehemently opposed to any form of religion (including Islam) that failed to comply with its understanding and practice of Islam. Boko Haram invaded schools and different communities, kidnapping young men and women as well as looting properties. According to the UNICEF 2018 report, Boko Haram is on record for kidnapping over 1000 children, including 276 school girls from Chibok, since 2013.[1] Since 2009, different political leaders in Nigeria declared ending Boko Haram insurgency their top priority. However, rather than being contained, this religious motivated terrorist organization developed a splinter organization which has aligned itself to an extension of ISIS in West Africa. Given the focus of the hostilities of these terrorist organizations on both Christians and Muslims, members of both religions are propelled to work together to end or diminish existing antagonism between them. It is reported that Muslims and Christians in the northeast areas of Nigeria (places most affected by Boko Haram militancy) have collaborated to support the needs of Christians and Muslims affected by the devastations and horrors from Boko Haram attacks.[2] Consequently, after decades of Muslim-Christian conflicts, there are today growing numbers of Muslim-Christian collaborations across the country that advocate for peaceful co-existence of Muslims and Christians in Nigeria. A new paradigm shift is thus emerging.

I Organizations working for Sustainable Muslim-Christian relations

The growing number of organizations with the mission of ameliorating or ending incidents of Muslim-Christian violent conflicts are established either by the government, religious organizations, NGOs or resulting from collaborations by all three organizations in different parts of Nigeria.³

With the erratic quest for and the consequent tumultuous response to the adoption of Sharia legal system in several northern states, the government of President Olusegun Obasanjo endorsed a government sponsored Christian-Muslim council, the Nigeria Inter-religious Council (NIREC), in 1999. It consisted of 50 members drawn equally from the Christian Association of Nigeria (CAN) and the Nigeria Supreme Council for Islamic Affairs (NSCIA). Among the objectives of the organization stated in Article 3 of its constitution are: 'To honestly and sincerely understand the true teachings of the two religions; promote dialogue between Christians and Muslims; inculcate moral, ethical, social and cultural values of the two faiths for the rebirth and rebuilding of a better society; to provide a forum for mutual co-operation and promotion of the welfare of all citizens in the nation.'⁴

Being government sponsored was both an asset and a liability of NIREC. Its political burdens manifested in the flawed attempts of NIREC to identify and address some of the fundamental roots of Christian-Muslim conflicts in Nigeria. Consequently, new organizations came into existence. IDFP (Interfaith Dialogue Forum for Peace), which is one of the recently established organizations⁵ is an advocacy group. It is a subsidiary of the King Abdullah Bin Abdulaziz International Centre for Interreligious and Intercultural Dialogue (KAICIID) in Vienna, Austria. It has focused on the following projects: establishment of a common forum for Christian and Muslim representatives to address interfaith issues; ongoing support for the creation of a code of conduct to regulate Muslim/Christian preaching through workshops and seminars; establishment of early warning networks in targeted areas in collaboration with the National Human Right Commission; social development programs at community levels through small grants to the IDFP member organizations.⁶

The Dialogue, Reconciliation and Peace (DREP) Centre in Jos, Plateau State is a good example of a faith-based organization working for healthy and sustainable dialogue between Christians and Muslims. Although it is owned by the Catholic Archdiocese of Jos, it works jointly with Muslims and Christians in Plateau state. It is enlisted as part of a global network of the United Religions Initiative (URI) with headquarters in San Francisco, California, USA.

The Interfaith Mediation Centre is headed by Imam Muhammad Ashafa and Pastor James Wuye, globally renowned not only because of the compelling stories of their pasts as religious bigots but also the transformation both went through after years of active interreligious antagonism and the positive impacts of their transformative experiences on their followers and admirers. These two individuals have become beacons of peace and interreligious collaboration between Muslims and Christians not only in northern Nigeria, but globally.[7]

The Kukah Centre is an NGO founded by Bishop Matthew Hassan Kukah, who has spent the greater part of his life as a cleric advocating for better appreciation of northern ethnic minorities as well as civil order in northern Nigeria between Muslims and Christians. The Kukah Centre states that interfaith dialogue 'is at the core of the Centre's work and involves actively promoting conversations among Nigeria's faith communities, as well as between leaders in faith and public policy.'[8] It also promotes civil discourse as well as 'active and engaged citizenry'.[9]

II A New Order of Muslim-Christian Relationships

From the list above of organizations actively engaged in advocating and promoting continued interreligious and intercultural engagements in different the parts of Nigeria, especially in areas that have experienced series of interreligious conflicts and violence, it is encouraging to know that Nigerians have meaningfully embraced sustainable approaches toward more peaceful co-existence and collaboration between Muslims and Christians, and indeed among all peoples of faith. Fr. Cornelius Afebu Omonokhua, executive secretary of NIREC, believes that 'To a great extent, these dialogues and interactions have been working for us.'[10] In addition, the records have shown that with the exception of the Boko Haram insurgency and the menace of Fulani Herdsmen, the frequency and devastation of Muslim-Christian conflicts have significantly dropped in Nigeria. Moreover, it is reported that today there are active collaborations between Muslims and Christians to address the Boko Haram insurgency. Different Islamic and Christian organizations are including training and sensitization of their adherents toward healthy and sustainable interreligious relations.[11]

The governments at both state and federal levels are now more proactively focused on mitigating further occurrences of interreligious conflicts, undoubtedly also to mitigate the negative economic impacts of such violence and their concomitant political disadvantages. Both the federal and state governments have prioritized the security of lives and properties, measures that have further enhanced the work and activities of individuals, groups, and organizations that are committed to promoting effective interreligious dialogue. The International Religious Freedom Report about Nigeria of 2018 mentions that 'Several states have laws requiring licenses for preachers, places of worship, and religious schools of registered religious groups.'[12] One of the consequences of some of the measures of the governments may be that of limiting the religious freedom of people whose activities might be interpreted as fomenting or inciting religious conflict. The federal security agencies are reported to have violently suppressed the peaceful demonstrations of members of the Islamic Movement of Nigeria (IMN) in 2018. The reason given by the government for its heavy-handed repression of the peaceful protest of those Shia Muslims was that the organization was inciting violent conflict.[13] The 'Nigeria 2018 International Religious Freedom Report' provides facts of government structures like commissions for peace created to facilitate ongoing dialogue between Christians and Muslims as well as interventions to resolve existing conflicts between Christians and Muslims in different parts of the country. These developments significantly promote and sustain healthy relationship among citizens of diverse religious and ethnic affiliations.

A Nigerian Islamic cleric, Imam Abubakar Abdullahi, was one of the recipients of the U.S. Department of State 2019 International Religious Freedom Award. He was honoured along with four other religious leaders from Brazil, Sudan, Iraq, and Cyprus for actively advocating religious freedom.[14] Imam Abdullahi, consistent with his belief in freedom of religion and respect for all lives, protected the lives of 262 Christians fleeing attacks from Muslim Fulani herdsmen in Barkin Ladi area of Plateau State.[15] Imam Abdullahi was convinced it was imperative and obligatory for him and his community to protect the Christians that fled to him and even offered to die on their behalf if the herdsmen insisted on killing them. The plot of land on which his mosque and home were built was given to him and his Muslim community by the Christians who owned the land.[16]

At the 2018 Parliament of World's Religions conference in Toronto, Canada, Rev. Abare Kallah's leadership and promotion of interreligious dialogue in Gombe, Bauchi State was recognized with the Paul Carus Award. Rev. Kallah is the founder of the Community Peace Dialogue and Interfaith Initiative, which has been responsible for building 58 Interfaith Peacemaker Teams (IPT) from 2015 to 2018 in and around the city of Gombe.[17]

III Conclusion

Since 1999 with the formation of NIREC and the long spell of violent conflicts between Christians and Muslims in different cities of Nigeria, there have been growing number of groups and individuals actively working for peace, collaboration, civility, and effective dialogue between Christians and Muslims. It is fair to conclude that although Nigerians bear the scars of Christian-Muslim conflicts as well as the horror of Boko Haram insurgency and more recently the violent attacks of Muslim Fulani Herdsmen, mutual collaborations and effective interreligious dialogue activities between Muslims and Christians have genuinely grown with positive social impacts and effects, especially in the areas of the country most affected by the conflicts and religiously motivated violence. There are programs and structures put in place by the different state governments to thwart possible indicators of religious motivated violence and interreligious conflict. Therefore, the collective energies of governments, religious organizations, NGOs and concerned individuals to both address and prevent incidents of religiously motivated violence and previously incessant Muslim-Christian conflicts are commendable. They need more public support and sincere commitment to their stated objectives.

There should be growing number of Imam Abdullahi and Rev. Kallah in different parts of Nigeria, especially in those parts of the country that have had first-hand experience of the darkness and horror of interreligious conflicts. It is therefore, imperative for enduring and effective interreligious dialogue, relations and better civil society, for more education and understanding of the religious other and the efficacy of genuine works of dialogue. Such education should become part of the core curriculum at all levels of education in Nigeria. Sadly, the religious education curricula currently in use are both confessional in orientation and catechetical in approach. Such curricula should focus more on religious education with intent of emphasizing the multi-religious landscape of Nigeria and the existing constitutional freedom of religion as well as underscoring inclusive religious pluralistic worldview and healthy intercultural and interreligious co-existence and collaboration. [18]

Notes

1. Stephanie Busari, 'UNICEF: Boko Haram has kidnapped more 1000 children in Nigeria', CNN. Retrieved on 2 November 2019. https://www.cnn.com/2018/04/13/africa/boko-haram-children-abduction-intl/index.html.
2. Patrick Eqwu, 'Nigeria's Interfaith Council Fosters Peaceful Christian-Muslim Relations', *National Catholic Reporter*, 11 November 2019, par. 12. https://www.ncronline.org/news/people/nigerias-interfaith-council-fosters-peaceful-christian-muslim-relations. Retrieved on 16 November 2019.
3. Chidiebere Ogbonna, 'The Role of the Church in Supporting Community Resilience Preventing and Countering Violent Extremism: The case of Nigeria' in Elias O. Opongo (ed.), *Religious Extremism and Violence in Africa- Reviewing the Practice of Intervention and Inter-Religious Dialogue*, Nairobi, Kenya: Hekima Institute of Peace Studies and International Relations Research Series, 2019, 36.
4. Cornelius Afebu Omonokhua, 'In search of One Nation Through NIREC', Catholic Secretariat of Nigeria. https://www.csnigeria.org/articledetail.php?tab=111. par. 5. Retrieved on 16 November 2019.
5. IDFP was established in February 2016, funded by KAICIID Dialogue Centre, Vienna. See Interfaith Dialogue Forum for Peace (IDFP), Best Practice of Peace. https://www.idfpnigeria.org/about-us/.
6. Interfaith Dialogue Forum for Peace, 14 June 2019 post. Facebook. https://www.facebook.com/IDFPNIGERIA/. Retrieved 16 November 2019. See also Interfaith Dialogue Forum for Peace, 2018 Annual Report. https://www.idfpnigeria.org/wp-content/uploads/2019/04/IDFP-REPORT.pdf.
7. Charles M. Sennott, 'A Pastor and an Imam Once Tried Kill Each Other – Now They Try to Heal Nigeria', Lifestyle & Belief of PRI. https://www.pri.org/stories/2014-03-10/pastor-and-imam-once-tried-kill-each-other-now-they-work-heal-nigeria. 10 March 2014. Retrieved 16 November 2019.
8. See 'About Us', The Kukah Centre. https://thekukahcentre.org/. Par. 2. Retrieved 16 November 2019.
9. The Kukah Centre, par. 2.
10. Patrick Eqwu, 'Nigeria's Interfaith Council Fosters Peaceful Christian-Muslim Relations', *National Catholic Reporter*, 11 November 2019, par. 6. https://www.ncronline.org/news/people/nigerias-interfaith-council-fosters-peaceful-christian-muslim-relations. Retrieved on 16 November 2019.
11. A good example is the Nasrulahi-l-Fatih Society (NASFAT), which runs training

program for its members to promote healthy interreligious relations. See 'NASFAT Trains Muslims on Good Inter-faith Relations', *The Nation*, 25 December 2018. https://thenationonlineng.net/nasfat-trains-muslims-good-inter-faith-relations/. Retrieved 19 November 2019.

12. See *International Religious Freedom Report* for 2018, 'Nigeria 2018 International Religious Freedom Report', United States Department of State, Bureau of Democracy, Human Rights, and Labour. https://www.state.gov/wp-content/uploads/2019/05/NIGERIA-2018-INTERNATIONAL-RELIGIOUS-FREEDOM-REPORT.pdf, 4. Retrieved on 16 November 2019.

13. *International Religious Freedom Report* for 2018, 5.

14. 2019 Awardees, 'International Religious Freedom Award Winners', U.S. Department of State. 16 July 2019. https://www.state.gov/international-religious-freedom-award-winners/. Retrieved 16 November 2019.

15. Bukola Adebayo, 'Muslim Cleric Who Hid Christians During Attacks Honored in the US', CNN. July 18, 2019. https://edition.cnn.com/2019/07/18/africa/nigeria-cleric-honored-intl/index.html. Retrieved 16 November 2019.

16. See 2019 Awardees, 'International Religious Freedom Award Winners,' par. 3.

17. See '2018 Parliament Awards: Rev. Abare Kallah, the Paul Carus Award, and the Path Toward Peace in Nigeria', Parliament of the World's Religions. Parliament Blog posted 04/08/2019. https://parliamentofreligions.org/blog/2019-09-13-1201/2018-parliament-awards-rev-abare-kallah-paul-carus-award-and-path-toward-peace?utm_source=Email%20Updates&utm_campaign=98330637eb-EMAIL_CAMPAIGN_2019_04_09_05_38_COPY_01&utm_medium=email&utm_term=0_5516d1b278-98330637eb-87813193&mc_cid=98330637eb&mc_eid=a684e1ee21. Retrieved December 8, 2019.

18. For more details on inclusive cultural and religious pluralism you may refer to one of my works. See Marinus C. Iwuchukwu, *Muslim-Christian Dialogue in Postcolonial Northern Nigeria: The Challenges of Inclusive Cultural and Religious Pluralism*. New York: Palgrave Macmillan publishers, 2013.

Hospitality and Mutuality in Egypt

JEAN DRUEL

This article is a reflection on my field observations and interactions with Egyptians students and scholars, both at the IDEO (Dominican Institute for Oriental Studies) and in our partner institutions in Cairo (two faculties in the University of al-Azhar, the Bureau of the Grand Imam, the World Association of al-Azhar Graduates, the Manuscript Institute of the Arab League and the American University). In the aftermath of the atrocities perpetrated by Daesh[1] the self-called Islamic State established in late 2006, young educated Muslims students in Cairo who do not want to quit Islam altogether are now reaching out to religious minorities and turn to contemporary human sciences as a means to re-appropriate Islam. This double-sided tendency is clearly observable in Cairo since 2014.

In the past years, I have witnessed a new trend among Islamic institutions seeking collaborations with IDEO. If our scholarship has always been respected, we had the feeling until recently that Islamic institutions were reluctant to engage with us in active partnerships. The first Islamic institution to officially contact us was the Tafseer Centre in Ryad, Saudi Arabia, a centre specialized in Qur'anic studies, who visited us in July 2017. Their director, Sheikh Abdulrahman Al Shehri came to the IDEO and told us that he had two problems. The first one is that none of the scholars in his centre masters a foreign language so that they have practically no access to non-Arabic research on the Qur'an, and the second problem is that whenever they contact Western scholars these are often less than cooperative because of their Saudi nationality and Salafi look. Sheikh Al Shehri asked us to help them be the link between Western scholars and them. This interesting meeting was followed by contacts from other

Islamic institutions: Al-Furqan Islamic Heritage Foundation (a Saudi-funded research centre in London), the Islamic Studies Laboratory at the IFAN (Institut fondamental d'Afrique noire, Dakar), the Arabic Manuscript Institute of the Arab League in Cairo, and the World Association of al-Azhar Graduates.

The case of al-Azhar is different but interesting. We have always had excellent relations with the Grand Imam's office but no actual joint projects, either with him or with the university or any other sister institution, until a group of students contacted us in 2015. They expressed their need for methodology classes in the human sciences. We began to organize small workshops in the IDEO's library, until the dean of their faculty (males' Faculty of Languages and Translation) formally asked us to stop until we had signed a formal agreement. It took us a year to achieve this, mainly because the dean of this faculty and the president of the university were blocking the process. It was only after the Grand Imam intervened that we could formally sign the agreement in 2016 and resume our workshops.

Thanks to a 500,000 € grant from the EU in 2018, we are now able to fund activities both with al-Azhar University and the Arab Manuscript Institute. As for the other institutions, the discussions are still ongoing. Obviously, institutions move more slowly than individuals.

I have also witnessed two interesting dynamics among younger Muslim students and scholars in Cairo. I cannot generalize to other cities in Egypt, or to all sectors of the Egyptian society, because I do not have a first-hand experience of these milieus. But if what I witness today is a premise of what is to spread to other sectors of society, then it is a real sign of hope.

The first one is the attitude of young Cairene university scholars towards religious diversity. Fifteen years ago, many Muslim students and scholars were quite ill at ease talking with Christian priests, or simply entering a priory or a church. They would either not think of doing so, or they would be afraid, not even thinking of asking whether it was possible. Some who were more daring or simply older, would come to us at the Dominican Institute which is located inside a priory, and share their interest in entering a church, just to see what it looks like inside.

The case of Amr Abdelaty Saleh, a then English-language student at the University of al-Azhar is significant. My predecessor Jean Jacques Pérennès met him by chance in 2003 at the mosque of al-Azhar. They began to talk and they finally organized a meeting at the Institute. When Amr arrived, he recalled that he panicked when he saw the word "monastery" (*dayr*) on the outside wall (the IDEO is hosted at the Dominican Priory). He simply turned back and called Jean Jacques to apologize that he had been busy and they agreed on a new appointment. This time, he told friends where he was going and asked them to call the police if they did not hear from him before a fixed hour. What he knew of "monasteries" is that they are places where black magic is performed. The case of Amr is anecdotal but probably not isolated. After completing his PhD at al-Azhar University, Amr is now completing a second PhD in a Pontifical University in Rome, on the image of Jesus in the works of the famous Muslim scholar al-Ghazali (d. 505/1111).

Ten years later, after 2014, Muslims would come and attend mass out of curiosity, browse our liturgical books, sign up for an open day at the priory, share their experience on our Facebook page (exposing themselves to their friends). On the occasion of an open day in the Dominican priory in Cairo in December 2017, I got to know about an institute for Coptic studies in Alexandria. I was impressed to realize that most of its scholars are Muslims who study the Coptic language, history and archaeology. Years ago, Muslims would fear that their Islam would be "contaminated" by too much proximity with Christians. This is clearly not the case anymore today. On the contrary, many come to us in order to enrich their vision of the world, and to expand their experience.

Similarly, there was a TV show fifteen years ago devoted to Bahá'ís. The tone was dramatic: the anchor-man was very aware that he was breaking a taboo. By contrast, when one of the leaders of the Egyptian Bahá'í community visited us in 2018, he was clearly not hiding any-more, even organizing Bahá'í events at the American University and inviting us to attend one of their services.

Recently, Egyptian filmmakers have made movies on the Egyptian Jews,[2] on Copts in Upper Egypt,[3] on the Egyptian Armenian community,[4] and on Copts affected with leper.[5] To be sure, these movies were not blockbusters, but they were projected in Cairo and have found their public.

My impression is that today, in younger educated milieus in Cairo, religious diversity is seen as a positive feature of Egyptian society and more and more people want to highlight it. Even more, diversity is seen as a way to enrich one's own religious and human experience.

The second sign of hope that I see today among young Cairene scholars is their willingness to study contemporary human sciences and apply them to religion. The older generations still have very strong reservations about analysing the Qur'an, the Islamic tradition or Islamic rites through contemporary human sciences (philosophy, sociology, critical history, psychology, hermeneutics) partly because they do not master these sciences and partly for ideological reasons. Until recently, it was almost impossible to read academic literature in the human sciences in Arabic. There were very few translations available and a very limited production in Arabic. The past few years have seen a dramatic increase in the number of good translations, published in the Maghreb and in Lebanon.

In the past, the lack of access to the human sciences was often reinforced by ideological arguments. Opponents argue that Islam is not a human phenomenon: it can never be analysed with human tools, and human sciences can only bring deception and misunderstanding. In the vision of many Muslims, both uneducated and educated, what they call "Islam" is a theoretical concept that was revealed by God to the Prophet along with the Qur'an. The much celebrated *What is Islam?* by Shahab Ahmed (Princeton University Press, 2016) points to the fact that there is no general agreement on the meaning of the term "Islam." Far from Ahmed's vision of Islam encompassing everything that has seen the light in the shadow of the Qur'an, for many believers, whatever Islam is, it is perfect and thoroughly divine. If we push the reflection a step further, we can probably infer that many Muslim scholars in Egypt today have a pre-Bacon non-empirical understanding of what truth is. For them, truth is a simple, binary judgement on facts and statements. Its simplicity makes it absolute. Islam is either absolutely true of false and its historical realizations are nothing but human noise or instrumentalization and studying these realizations is a loss of time that says nothing of what Islam is.

There are two consequences to this popular understanding of truth. First, Islam is not questionable with human tools, and second, Islam is completely innocent of whatever historical realization is implemented in its name. This traditional vision is still extremely prevalent in universities and research centres in Egypt, not only among uneducated believers. To put it simply, many think that Daesh is not Islamic in any way. It is only the by-product of the West's and Israel's continuous efforts to destabilize Arab and Islamic countries.

However, in 2017 it was on the insistent request of a group of students from al-Azhar University that we organized a seminar devoted to human sciences applied to religion. We planned five sessions, each devoted to a different approach of religion: psychology, philosophy, law, sociology and logic. We were absolutely amazed by the warm welcome this seminar found among the patrons of our library. We had to organize a sharp selection and could finally welcome only forty students out of the eighty who applied, because of the capacity of our seminar hall.

The French ministry of Interior offers each year PhD scholarships in religious sciences. In the course of the past five years, there have always been three or four Egyptian candidates from al-Azhar University who express their desire to learn how to apply the human sciences to the religion.

The questions that some of these young Muslim scholars ask us can be summarized as follows: how can one be fully liberal in one's education and deeply committed to one's religion? I came to realize that this is the way most of these scholars in al-Azhar University see us, liberal and religious at the same time, which for them sounds as an oxymoron. I believe that there is clearly a counter-Daesh effect here. For many young Muslims, if Daesh represents Islam, then they prefer to declare themselves not Muslim anymore, and "atheism" is clearly growing in the Egyptian educated milieus. I put it between brackets because what they actually mean is rather a non-observant religiosity, not atheism *per se*. Others who do not want to go so far as declaring themselves non-believers, seek an answer in diversity, which Daesh clearly condemns, and in contemporary human sciences, which traditional scholarship ignores. The Islamic uniformity that Daesh preaches literally kills people, and young educated Muslims in Cairo who do not want to quit Islam thus seek refuge in religious diversity and in contemporary human sciences.

Reflecting back on the past years, it appears that the year 2014 was a turning point in the relations between IDEO and Islamic institutions and Muslim scholars. That year witnessed a peak in the atrocities committed by Daesh, which probably pushed many Muslims to speak out and condemn more vocally what was being committed in the name of Islam. That same year, on December 3 & 4, the Grand Imam Ahmad al-Tayyib held an international symposium on "Confronting extremism and terrorism" during which he acknowledged that Daesh was an Islamic problem (against international pressures to declare Daesh apostate), and that Muslim scholars should be held responsible for the education of "our children who went astray." I am not suggesting that this speech caused students, scholars and institutions to seek help at the IDEO, but only that the year 2014 corresponded to a turning point where Muslims, both individually and collectively, began to explore new solutions to their problems, including collaborations with non-Muslim scholars and institutions. And that is certainly a sign of hope for Muslim-Christian relations in Egypt.

Afterword
Before sending this article for publication, I asked above-mentioned Amr Abdelaty Saleh if he agreed that his name appears here. He read the article and disagreed with almost every line in it. Not about his story with the IDEO but about my interpretation of what happened in 2014 and the reason why more Muslim individuals and institutions would now seek collaboration with us. It was extremely important for me that an article that deals with dialogue would give a voice to the very ones it would talk about! Amr's first concern was that my article could imply that Muslims would come to the IDEO out of a feeling of guilt before Daesh's atrocities, not out of a genuine desire to meet the other, which is not what I intended, although I understand that it could be implied. His second point is that we, at the IDEO, have also changed. Not only is the new generation of brothers more fluent in Arabic at an academic level, but many of our prejudices have disappeared. Amr recalled that in 2003 brothers, including me, would often show aggressivity towards Islam and bluntly ask newcomers to the Institute to account for the Prophet's young wives or military campaigns. Also, he reminded me that I was precisely appointed as the director in 2014, meaning that a fully fluent Arabic speaker was now in charge, which may also explain why Islamic institutions could more easily seek collaboration. Lastly, he added that there may be many factors that can explain the desire of students and institutions to seek collaboration, from a genuine desire of the students to learn up-to-date research methodology to a more interested

quest for a steppingstone to Western universities; and for institutions, from a true will to collaborate to a mere political agenda to show off as being "open-minded" in their own countries. All very pragmatic reasons that have nothing to do with a renewed consciousness caused by Daesh.

Reading this article again from the beginning, I decided not to modify it but to add this afterword and leave it to the reader to judge. As usual in interreligious dialogue, the process behind the text is more important than the text itself, and when Amr left the Institute after this exciting discussion he told me how moved he was that we both had enough confidence in the other to share our insights and disagree. This alone is, I believe, a sign of hope. It requires two things that are usually missing in today's world between believers of different religions: time and friendship.

Notes

1. Daesh", or *Dā'ish* in Arabic, is acronym of *al-Dawla al-Islāmiyya fī al-'Irāq wa-l-Shām*, the "Islamic State in Iraq and the Levant". First established in 2006 in Iraq in opposition to the existing State, it was finally declared to be the "Caliphate" in 2014.
2. *Jews of Egypt*, 2012, by Amir Ramses
3. *The Virgin, the Copts and me*, 2012, by Namir Abdel Messeeh
4. *We are Egyptian Armenians*, 2016, by Waheed Sobhi, Eva Dadrian, and Hanan Ezzat
5. *Yomeddine*, 2018, by Abu Bakr Shawky

Part Four: Hope for the Future of Muslim-Christian Relations

A Shared Desire for a Universal Vision

DANIEL A. MADIGAN, S.J.

Islam and Christianity are what Miroslav Volf calls 'contending particular universalisms'. To escape that inherent contentiousness we tend either to discount each other's universal claims, or to gloss over our particularities and claim that all religions are 'really' the same. Neither strategy succeeds and we despair of ever emerging from our confrontations. Signs of hope emerge when we acknowledge both the particularities of our traditions and the profound shared desire for a universal vision. Contending *against one other can be transformed into contending* together *with the great questions of God and humanity.*

To search for signs of hope in Muslim-Christian dialogue might seem like a fool's errand. We can find causes for despair delivered daily to our doorsteps, and hourly to our screens in blaring headlines with full-colour illustrations – not just news of attacks on one another, but ever more strident affirmations of the impossibility of our being reconciled, or even of being able to arrive at a shared understanding of human life under God. Discerning signs of hope in this context will be like recognizing the signs of the Kingdom: they sprout like small seedlings, all too easily crushed, in need of care and cultivation. Indeed, every sign of hope *is* a sign of the Kingdom.

Islam and Christianity are, to use Miroslav Volf's term, 'contending particular universalisms.'[1] They are two among the many visions of human flourishing that understand themselves to apply to all human beings – hence 'universalism.' Nonetheless, they are rooted in appeals to very specific historical and textual origins, and they are lived out in various concrete social and cultural situations – hence 'particular.' Because they make universal claims, because they are not identical, and because they have to be lived out in particular times and places, they will inevitably exist in some contention with one another. But must this contention be cause for despair? Can we find hope in it? Volf's concept can help us map the contours of our fears and disappointments, but it also enables us to pinpoint the opportunities that offer us hope.

Signs of hope are not just isolated positive events. Something gives us hope because we recognize it as having grown out of an opportunity that is constant or at least repeatable. If one person or group can capitalize on such an opportunity, so will others be able to as well. The signs of hope are no guarantee of future achievement, of course, and they may long remain outnumbered by the many missed opportunities. However, in spite of their fragility, they keep pointing us toward opportunity.

From its emergence in the 7th century CE, Islam has seen itself as a corrective to Christianity, as a reiteration of the universal divine plan for human flourishing. It does not present itself as a new religion, but rather as the re-establishment of the original religion that has existed from the beginning, and of which Judaism and Christianity are examples – even if Islam holds that they have needed to be purified of certain extraneous elements. Islam could be seen as a reform movement within the religious world of Late Antiquity, shaped as that world was by Christianity and Judaism among other traditions. As a movement Islam proposes a substantial re-reading of the Abrahamic, Mosaic, Christian tradition that had developed in biblical and post-biblical literature and practice. For believing Muslims, it is not simply a human reform movement, of course, but God's reform – first as a restoration of what Arab religion had disfigured of Abrahamic worship; and second as a warning to Christians and Jews that their grasp of and adherence to the revelation God had given them was seriously lacking. So contention is a founding aspect of the relationship between Muslims and Christians, in the sense that it could be said each sees the other as heretical: each claims to have the true and correct understanding of who Jesus is and what God intended to do through him. We do not encounter one another as, for example, Buddhism and Christianity might – as traditions that grew up in isolation from one another and have no specific knowledge of the other enshrined in their sacred texts and traditions.

It is difficult to see, therefore, how we can hope to overcome the fundamental contentiousness of our relationship. We have both tried to dissolve it in various ways, first by denying universality, then by denying particularity.

I Denying Universality

In a classic trope of medieval polemics, Christian writers claimed that it was clear from the Qur'an itself that Muḥammad was sent only to the pagan Arabs who had not previously been addressed by God. Since the Qur'an prides itself on being in Arabic, observed Paul of Antioch, a Melkite Bishop writing in the 13th century, and since Arabic is not the language of the Christians, it is clear that, even if they were to grant that Muḥammad was from God, he was not sent to them.[2] Muslims in turn claimed that, according to the Qur'an, Jesus was sent to the people of Israel (Q 43:59). Later, when the gospel texts were more widely known, Muslims would be also able to point to Jesus' own sayings to this effect (e.g., Mt 15:24). Muḥammad, on the other hand was clearly sent to all people, according to Paul's respondents, like Ibn Taymiyya (d. 1328): 'All religious groups have known that Muḥammad summoned Jews and Christians to faith in him and declared that God sent him to them.'[3] Even if Jesus' mission had been to all humanity, goes the complaint, it had clearly failed. His followers had changed his religion – and so it was necessary for God to send a new prophet who would succeed in the task of reestablishing the pristine worship of God and the rule of justice which follows from the obedience of faith. The mission of that prophet would encompass both the already-scriptured people, who had fallen away, and people who had not yet received a prophetic messenger.

This kind of denial that an *earlier* tradition really is universal is a supersessionist tactic. When universality is denied to a *later* tradition, it is an attempt to marginalize it. Either way, the contentiousness is not resolved, since no tradition with a claim to universality can accept to be superseded or marginalized in this way. Universality could be denied to *both* traditions, of course, as pluralist theologies tend to do. Any universalist vision is identified as a form of absolutism – a kind of power play – which is then denounced. However, that universal vision is not so easily displaced, because it is not just a replaceable element in a system of thought. Rather it is the horizon against which everything is perceived, and as such for believers it carries an existential ultimacy that cannot simply be yielded to an Enlightenment critique of absolutes. In denying universality to any religious vision, many pluralist theologies exercise what we might call a 'balkanizing' tendency. The different particular visions of what constitutes the right relationship between God and humanity are permitted to, as it were, carve out their own spheres of influence, as long as they respect the borders of other visions and do not advance expansionist claims. Even if such a policy were functional at the level of ideas, when it comes to the particularity of social contexts and political structures, religious balkanization is no more successful at resolving contentiousness than it was in the eponymous Balkans.

II Denying Particularity

If universality is denied to the other in order to claim victory, or at least to negotiate a truce, so also can particularity be denied in an attempt to reduce contentiousness. The idea that all religions at a fundamental level teach the same thing is the stuff of popular books and television series on religions.[4] The particularities of religious affirmations and practices are elided as being no more significant than differences in language. The 'objective scholar' of religion claims that, whatever words particular traditions may be using, they are 'in fact' expressing the same universal human faith. This kind of homogenizing might be reassuring to the non-religious person nervous about the sometimes bizarre variety of human religious practice, and the apparently incompatible claims of believers. However, the believer herself might reasonably object to being told she does not really mean what she says, and that what she 'really means' is the same as what everyone else 'really means'. The 'objective scholar' is in effect trying to replace the other particular universalisms with what might seem to her to be a universal universalism, but which in the end proves to be just as particular as the others – just as much shaped by the historical moment, the prevailing culture, the contemporary apprehension of the good.

III Bowing to Reality and Reaping the Fruits

These strategies of denying universality and denying particularity seem to offer little hope for reducing contention between the 'contending particular universalisms' of Islam and Christianity. We will have to live with all three elements: universalism, particularity and contention. The question before us is whether, by acknowledging and respecting universality and particularity rather than denying them, contention can be made fruitful rather than destructive. Signs of hope will not be found where we have agreed to abandon the universality of our respective visions for humanity, or where we have agreed to gloss over the historical and cultural particularity of the way they arose and have been lived. On the contrary, hope emerges where our contention consists in exploring and interrogating together our particularities, and in learning to recognize in the other the desire for and commitment to the same kind of positive universal vision as we have.

After this rather extended introduction, I propose some examples where the ability to hold the universalism and particularity together makes for a productive and hopeful kind of contention. However, it must be realized that each moment of opportunity can also be misused. For example, the fact that Muslims in the United States are a small minority makes possible a kind of Muslim-Christian relationship that is not warped by the considerations of power that are in play in Pakistan. At the same time that same minority status can be exploited by the Christian party to exact 'payback' for perceived injustices done to Christians in Pakistan.

IV Acknowledging Particularity
4.1. Ideals and realities

When universalist visions contend with one another, they are apt to focus on their pristine ideals rather than on the more mixed record of their faltering attempts to embody those ideals in particular circumstances, and to give them cultural and political form in the real world. We live in an historical moment when it is increasingly difficult for Christians to nourish the illusion of moral superiority through which lens the West has usually regarded Muslims. The shameless abuses of power, the naked ambition, the craven compromises, and the self-serving corruption in our politics are daily on display. The revelations of the #MeToo movement and the investigations into clerical and other institutional abuse of the vulnerable have shattered the façade of virtue from behind which we usually launch our moralizing attacks on others. The unabashed re-emergence of chauvinist nationalisms and racist supremacism rekindles the bitter history of such ills that we had hoped had reached its nadir in the twentieth century.

For Muslims too, this historical moment is one of reckoning: with the moral bankruptcy of terrorism and the savage predations of the so-call Islamic State; with the inability to put an end to sectarian hatreds, tribalism, autocracy and military repression, and so to establish equitable societies. Then there are the evils we are complicit in together: the despoiling of our environment; the arms trade; the crushing injustice of the world financial systems; the human trafficking and the exploitation of migrant labour; the drug trade; the shameful neglect of the world's poor.

Ironically, perhaps, this bleak moment presents us with a major opportunity: our pretensions to moral superiority have been shown to be empty. If each community can honestly admit its failures rather than try to maintain that it only has a speck in its eye compared to the plank in the other's, then there is hope for something new to happen in Muslim-Christian relations.[5] Every time we drop the mask and admit the truth to each other is a small sign of hope.

4.2. New academic possibilities
A further opportunity to make a hopeful move is offered us in the increasing number of Muslims who are now active in the Western academy, not just in the sciences and professions, as has long been the case, but in the humanities, and in particular in the study of Islam. Somewhat over the protestations of Orientalist establishments, Islamic studies in parts of Europe and the United States are finding the way to be both scientific and confessional, functioning in tandem with traditional faculties of Christian theology. Muslim researchers whose intellectual formation has been in Western schools and universities recognize the particularity of, say, the Arabic-Islamic intellectual tradition, and are without any defensiveness able to find ways to express its universal vision within the different particularity of new paradigms.[6]

Biblical studies has had to re-learn how to approach scripture not just as a complex cultural artefact but as the sacred text of a believing community.

So too Western Qur'anic studies is schooling itself to move beyond the historical-critical obsession with origins, borrowings and redactions in order to see the Qur'an not as merely a derivative document but as a self-aware and self-confident voice in the polyphony of Late Antique religion. One can see this transformation most clearly, perhaps, in the development of the International Qur'anic Studies Association, formed by a group of Muslim, Christian and Jewish scholars of the Qur'an in 2014.[7] IQSA's standard of scholarship and its international reach are striking, but so too is its ability to take the Qur'an seriously as scripture, and therefore also as a source for theology. My own work on the Qur'an is at least in part a theological exercise, and it has been encouraging to see emerging Muslim scholars engaging positively with it in that vein.[8]

4.3. Scripture or the Word
Presuming the universality of the category of scripture has long been a major block to fruitful Muslim-Christian understanding, and too much energy has been spent on arguments about textual authenticity. It is gradually coming to be realized that the difference between our traditions lies not in the proof-texts we can cite, but more fundamentally in what we identify as the defining historical moment of God's address to humanity. We share almost universally a belief in speech as an essential attribute of God; our particularity lies in where in history we see the defining moment of that speaking: the event of Qur'an (God's speech in clear Arabic, transmitted and interpreted by the Prophet), or the event of Jesus (God's Word expressed in flesh-and-blood, in a human life, death and resurrection). For mutual theological understanding, this somewhat unexpected parallel is an essential insight, and it is gradually gaining more currency, opening the way to more sophisticated understandings of each other.[9] In one sense, theological engagements are contentious. However, they are not a struggle for superiority, but rather a mutual probing and challenging in service to our search for truth.

One of the most sustained theological dialogues of Muslim and Christian scholars has been the series of four- or five-day annual meetings called The Building Bridges Seminar – we use the singular, since we try to maintain a continuity of participation over the years – established and developed by the Archbishops of Canterbury 2002–2012 and stewarded since then by Georgetown University.[10] It is worth considering the trajectory of this seminar under our rubric of 'contending particular universalisms'. From its beginning in the wake of the September 2001 attacks, the seminar has met under the shadow of constant, often violent, contention between Muslims and Christians: we still have not seen the end of the war in Iraq that was just beginning as the seminar's second meeting took place in Qatar in 2003; we have met twice in the tortured city of Sarajevo; our choice of venue has been determined not only positively by the generosity of hosts, but also negatively at times by the politics of suspicion and exclusion.

It has been an act of hope to sustain our study together over these decades, and also an act of love, for the community of scholars that has made up the seminar is nourished by the friendship that develops when people explore their sacred texts in each other's company. From an early concern to find commonalities and minimize difference, we have developed a greater capacity to explore each tradition's particularities. From somewhat external issues – law and rights, tradition and modernity, religion and science – we have developed sufficient trust in each other to be able to explore questions at the very heart of our faith and of our traditions' disagreements – sin and salvation, prayer, naming God. We turned explicitly to the question of the unity of God only after fifteen years. It was worth the wait. We managed to resist a move to reconceive the Trinity in 'the only islamically acceptable way' – i.e., to dissolve our particularity – and we persevered in exploring how both traditions had grappled with similar questions about God that follow necessarily from our belief not only in the unity of God but in the engagement of God with what is not God. We came away from that meeting with a new appreciation for the seriousness with which both our traditions had grappled with this foundational question.

Although the seminar is avowedly academic, its method is based on small-group study, as much as possible of scriptural texts. In order to avoid the tendency to gloss over difference, each day is devoted to study of only one tradition's texts on a question. The particularities are thus respected, yet in conversation over four days we come to understand how those particularities fit into a universal vision that embraces the whole. We contend with one another, certainly, but in the sense that we find ourselves contending together with the great questions of God and humanity and the broader creation.

V Acknowledging Universalism

Recognizing the particularity of our visions need not rule out a recognition of their universal nature. That very universality means that there will probably be some overlap between them. However, more important than the simple recognition of shared elements of the vision is the recognition of its universal reach, of its sense of cohesive unity and concern for all. Contending with one another about the particularities of our visions from within a recognition of a shared universal human concern leads to a more fruitful and hopeful engagement, even if it is no less complex. We see in the working together of Muslim and Christian feminist scholars, for example, a fundamentally shared desire for gender justice even in the midst of quite diverse particular cultural and political visions. The recognition of that shared foundational passion opens hopeful cross-fertilizations. A fine example would be the 'Muslima theology' of Jerusha Tanner Lamptey (now Rhodes) of Union Theological Seminary, New York, on religious pluralism and on comparative feminist theology.[11] Collaborative theologizing like this and like the Building Bridges Seminar offers the hope that, with a long-term commitment to patient study together there is a real possibility, not that we will negotiate an agreed settlement between Islam and Christianity, but that by taking each other's questions and challenges seriously we will allow ourselves to be led closer to the truth.

Notes

1. Miroslav Volf and Matthew Croasmun, For the Life of the World: Theology that Makes a Difference, Grand Rapids, MI: Brazos Press, 2019, 95–107.
2. The text of Paul's letter along with a more developed later version, both of which elicited extensive responses from some of the most significant Muslim scholars of the period, can be found in Rifaar Ebied and David Thomas (eds.), *Muslim-Christian Polemic During the Crusades: the Letter from the People of Cyprus and Ibn Abī Ṭālib al-Dimashqī's Response*, Leiden: Brill, 2005.
3. Ibn Taymiyya (d. 1328), *A Muslim Theologian's Response to Christianity*, translated and introduced by Thomas F. Michel, Ann Arbor: Caravan Books, 1984, p. 154.
4. See Sigal Samuel's insightful treatment of one such series: 'Reza Aslan and the Risks of Making Religion Relatable,' *The Atlantic*, March 12, 2017. https://www.theatlantic.com/

international/archive/2017/03/reza-aslan-cnn-believer-make-religion-relatable/
5. See Daniel Madigan, 'Our Next Word in Common: Mea Culpa?' in Yazid Said and Lejla Demiri (eds), *The Future of Interfaith Dialogue: Muslim-Christian Encounters through 'A Common Word'*, Cambridge: CUP, 2018, 177–191.
6. I think particularly of places of which I have direct experience in Paderborn, Tübingen and Edinburgh. One small example of such a work would be Abdul Rahman Mustafa, 'Ibn Taymiyyah & Wittgenstein on Language', *The Muslim World* 108 (2018), 465–491.
7. https://iqsaweb.wordpress.com The association grew out of year-long project by 25 scholars convened by Gabriel Said Reynolds at Notre Dame to comment on a selection of 50 passages from the Qur'an, using all the methods – literary, philological, theological, epigraphical – appropriate to scripture study. Mehdi Azaiez et al. (eds.), *The Qur'an Seminar Commentary: A Collaborative Study of 50 Qur'anic Passages* (Berlin: De Gruyter, 2016), Open Access.
8. See particularly Daniel Madigan, *The Qur'ān's Self-Image: Writing and Authority in Islam's Scripture*, Princeton: PUP, 2001.
9. See Daniel Madigan, 'The Gospel of John as a Structure for Muslim-Christian Understanding,' in Daniel Crowther et al., (eds.), *Reading the Bible in Islamic Context: Qur'anic Conversations*, New York: Routledge, 2018, 253–270.
10. The reports, videos and publications of the seminars are available at https://buildingbridges.georgetown.edu .
11. Jerusha Tanner Lamptey, *Never Wholly Other: a Muslima Theology of Religious Pluralism*, New York: OUP, 2014; and *Divine words, female voices: Muslima Explorations in Comparative Feminist Theology*, New York: OUP, 2018.

A Shared Culture of Justice and Reconciliation

ASMA AFSARUDDIN

On the surface of things, there is considerable reason to be pessimistic about the future trajectory of Christian-Muslim relations. Extremist rhetoric and behaviour in parts of the Muslim-majority world, manifested by militant groups like ISIS and the Taliban, continue to raise concern. In Christian-heritage societies in the West, powerful extremist groups continue to incite anti-immigration sentiment and blatant Islamophobia in significant parts of Europe and the United States. These are hardly positive auguries. This essay argues, however, that such a bleak picture does not take into consideration people of good will in these societies who subvert such patterns through their concerted daily efforts to promote better understanding of and communication with "the other." They refuse to give in to hate and cultivate instead a culture of justice and reconciliation. They provide us with hope – a desideratum in both the Muslim and Christian traditions.

Present global circumstances look dark and bleak – the rise of right-wing political groups; an increase in religious bigotry and violent extremism in many parts of the world; continuing climate change and environmental degradation; and the attrition of civility in public discourses, among others – are almost enough to make one lose hope in humanity. Certainly, this is the inevitable conclusion one would arrive at if one only focused on the media and its representation of current events. But what often gets left out of such frequently sensationalist coverage of current events are the dogged efforts of many people of good will who challenge such dominant narratives and establish an opposite paradigm of reconciliation and optimism. Many of them draw inspiration from the deep reserves of their religious traditions.

Here I focus on contemporary Muslim initiatives to model and nurture peaceful relations in a fractious world that allow us to imagine a different and hopeful future for humankind, especially in the context of Muslim-Christian relations. These initiatives are grouped under three main rubrics: justice, Qur'anic hermeneutics and interfaith activism.

I Justice, justice, and justice!

If there is one cardinal virtue that Muslims are expected to promote and adhere to without fail, it is justice. The importance of justice is firmly established in the Qur'an and hadith, the two main sources of Islamic ethics, morality and law. Muslims are expected to enjoin what is good and prevent what is wrong. They are therefore exhorted by their foundational religious texts to be always socially and communally engaged, because this struggle – in Arabic *jihad* – to combat wrongdoing and establish in this world justice in all its facets, is a fundamental religious duty.

In the Qur'an, this duty is furthermore intimately connected with being a moderate and "balanced" community. In Qur'an 2:143, the Arabic term *umma wasat* (literally: "a middle community/nation") is applied to righteous Muslims as a collectivity. If we look at a cross-section of classical Muslim exegeses of this critical term, we find that the overwhelming majority of exegetes understood "moderation" to inhere in being just and avoiding extremes in one's behaviour and beliefs. Thus, well-known classical Qur'an commentators like Muqatil b. Sulayman (d. 767), al-Tabari (d. 923) and al-Razi (d. 1210) say that moderation (*wasat*) implies above all adherence to justice and temperance ('*adl*).[1]

Moderation (and, therefore, being just) as an essential characteristic of all righteous people is furthermore indicated in Qur'an 5:66. In this verse, we find the Arabic term *umma muqtasida* which similarly refers to a "moderate and balanced community," here in relation to the Abrahamic faith communities. Taking their cue from this verse, the ecumenical or more inclusivist Muslim exegetes in the pre-modern period recognized moderation in all righteous practitioners of the Abrahamic faiths, who acknowledged their common spiritual kinship, came to the aid of one another, and were generally gentle and respectful in their mutual interactions.[2] The Qur'an therefore articulates what today we may recognize as religious pluralism within an Abrahamic context, according to which Judaism and Christianity are considered as kindred religions, particularly on the basis of shared values and praxis. Such inclusivist views appear to have been more common in the first two centuries of Islam. However, they became more attenuated in subsequent centuries due to conflictual encounters with Christian Europe in the pre-modern period, culminating in the European colonization of much of the Muslim world. Nevertheless, this early historical strand exists as a stark reminder for Muslims that their faith tradition contains the building blocks for fashioning in our times pluralist, peaceful, and, above all, just societies that respect everyone's religious commitments.

The word *jihad*, as we know, has been and continues to be horribly misused in the contemporary world by militant groups in Muslim-majority societies. The reason why the rhetoric of these militant groups unfortunately resonates with some segments of the global Muslim population is because many of these people live in politically and socially degraded circumstances. The rhetoric of liberation and self-determination – which militant groups promise them – appears to offer them an appealing alternative to their current predicament. A few are also induced to resort to armed violence to right the wrongs that have been inflicted on them, whether actual or perceived. The adoption of terror tactics by these misguided groups has come to define the meaning of *jihad* for most Westerners. But jihad divorced from just objectives and just means to achieve them is not *jihad* at all and represents a travesty of the highest Islamic ideals. The Qur'an (5:8) says: "Let not the hatred of others toward you cause you to deviate from justice. Behave justly – that is nearer to true piety." Such scriptural counsel is lost on these militant groups, consumed as they are by rancour and a desire for revenge.

Justice is also recognized as an essential value within Christianity. Within Catholicism, in particular, striving towards social justice received special emphasis during Vatican II and became enshrined as one of the seven basic tenets of Catholic social teaching after the 1960s. This development brought Christians much closer to Muslims in terms of their moral commitments to the larger society and, indeed, to the world.

The renewed emphasis on the universal value of justice today allows for interfaith coalitions to be formed that can effectively challenge gross infractions on human dignity in the form of continuing impoverishment, political oppression, and denial of access to socio-economic opportunities, among others. This kind of socially-engaged activism is *jihad* in its highest form – in which all humans of good will can take part to promote peaceful coexistence and global welfare, especially in the face of intolerance and violent manifestations of bigotry.

II Developing a Qur'anic Hermeneutics of Interfaith Relations

In a number of academic and popular venues today, a new hermeneutics of interfaith relations that draws upon past exegesis of the Qur'an often to put a new spin on them is becoming quite evident. According to this modern hermeneutic trend, many verses in the Qur'an that have a bearing on interfaith relations can be read with fresh eyes today in the context of our own socio-historical circumstances while yet remaining faithful to their actual wording and semantic landscape.

For example, a general injunction to engage with all peoples everywhere, irrespective of faith, ethnicity, and culture so as to engender mutual knowledge and understanding may be extrapolated from Qur'an 49:13. At the basic semantic level, this verse can be understood to advocate that humans should pro-actively "get to know one another" irrespective of one's backgrounds, and to remind us that individuals find esteem before God only on the basis of piety. In our own times, this verse is understood to be highly significant within a holistic discussion of Qur'anic perspectives on dialogic encounters. Because of the more parochial circumstances of their own time, medieval exegete however, typically tended to gloss the Arabic verb *ta'arafu* contained in this verse to mean learning about each other's tribal and similar affiliational backgrounds in order to establish bonds of kinship and affection. In explaining *ta'arafu*, al-Tabari, for example, glosses it as commanding people to get to know one another so that they may discover their bonds of kinship. He warns that knowledge of such kinship is not meant to induce any sense of superiority but rather "to bring you closer to God, for indeed only the most pious among you is the most honourable."[3]

Today we can expand the exegetical reach of the verb *ta'arafu* in this verse to extend beyond our blood-relatives so as to include all the co-residents of the global village which we are now beginning to regard as our shared home, thus realizing more fully the pluralist potential of this verse. In our contemporary circumstances, Qur'an 49:13 may be understood as representing the overall objective of interfaith and intercultural conversations – to broaden the common ground we inhabit as human beings and to learn about one another as inhabitants of different countries, cultures, and faith communities, with an appreciation for these differences that enrich our lives.

Another case in point is provided by the reinterpretation of the Qur'anic phrase *kalimat sawa'* in Qur'an 3:64 offered in what has now become widely known as *A Common Word*, a statement issued by 138 Muslim scholars and clerics in 2007.[4] It was addressed to Christian religious leaders and communities representing various denominations (with the exclusion initially of the evangelical Protestants) in 2007 and has received considerable attention in religious circles worldwide for drawing attention to the common theological ground between Muslims and Christians. The title *A Common Word Between You and Us* given to the statement reflects a contemporary translation of the Arabic phrase *kalimat sawa'* in Qur'an 3:64. The phrase in turn was further amplified by the Muslim signatories to refer to "love of God and love of neighbour" as the commandment held in common with Christians. The introductory paragraph reads as follows:

Muslims and Christians together make up well over half of the world's population. Without peace and justice between these two religious communities, there can be no meaningful peace in the world. The future of the world depends on peace between Muslims and Christians.

The basis for this peace and understanding already exists. It is part of the very foundational principles of both faiths: love of the One God, and love of the neighbour. These principles are found over and over again in the sacred texts of Islam and Christianity. The Unity of God, the necessity of love for Him, and the necessity of love of the neighbour is thus the common ground between Islam and Christianity.

Pre-modern exegetes usually understood the phrase *kalimat sawa'* as a broad reference to "a word of justice", a locution which in itself is open to interpretation. Justice is variously interpreted as "sincerity" by Muqatil, as "upright" and an assertion of the oneness of God by al-Tabari and al-

Zamakhshari (d. 1144); as "fair" and "equitable" by al-Razi, Ibn Kathir (d. 1373), and Muhammad 'Abduh (d. 1905).[5] With interpretive creativity, the modern signatories to *A Common Word* statement may be regarded as having distilled these various significations of justice into the pithy commandment "Love God and your neighbour." What after all could be more upright, sincere, just, and common than this commandment which resonates immediately with Abrahamic communities, and reaching even further, with all religious and ethical people?

In the wake of its proclamation in 2007, the *Common Word* statement has led to several high-level meetings between Muslim and Christian religious leaders, academics and inter-faith activists. The first was held at the Yale Divinity School in July 2008, where Muslim and primarily Protestant theologians discussed at length the two themes of the *Common Word* statement. A highly significant letter which articulated a very favourable response to the statement following this meeting was signed by three hundred prominent Protestant theologians and scholars and subsequently published in the *New York Times*.[6] The second meeting was hosted by the University of Cambridge in October, 2008 which culminated in a meeting with the then Archbishop of Canterbury Rowan Williams in London. The third high-level meeting took place at the Vatican in Rome on November 4-6, 2008 between 60 Muslim and Catholic scholars and religious leaders, which was constituted as the first Seminar of the Catholic-Muslim Forum that continues till today. Since 2008, several follow-up meetings have taken place at Georgetown University in Washington DC, as well as spin-off meetings at Oxford University, Heythrop College in London and at Mater Dei University in Dublin, Ireland. The *Common Word* statement may therefore be regarded as a seminal inter-faith document of our time that has potentially galvanized a new era of Muslim-Christian relations founded on common ground rooted in the scriptures of the two communities. Other inter-faith initiatives have also been born in the aftermath of September 11 that are directly or indirectly the result of the Common Word project.

III Interfaith Activism in the Face of Islamophobia: Impact upon Muslim-Christian Relations

In his best-selling book *The God Delusion,* the Oxford biologist and self-confessed atheist Richard Dawkins portrays Islam as "analogous to a carnivorous gene complex."[7] Hiding behind this turgid and inscrutable statement is a deep animus toward Islam and Muslims. Unfortunately, Dawkins is not exceptional in his views. He represents a growing trend in contemporary Western societies of a virulent strain of anti-Islamic sentiment, known as Islamophobia, that is not about to go away any time soon. Islamophobia went into overdrive after September 11 when Islam and Muslims regularly began to be equated with terror and terrorists in influential circles. The controversial and highly provocative "Clash of Civilizations" thesis first propounded by Samuel Huntington in 1993 began to be discussed again with renewed vigour in the post-September 11 milieu. As is well-known, Huntington had provocatively argued in the 1990s that the fault lines of conflict in the future would be along civilizational and religious lines, with Islamic civilization in particular set on a collision course with the Western one.[8]

As might be expected, his thesis has provoked much criticism from a number of historians and specialists in Islam who have underscored his poor knowledge of an assumed monolithic Islamic world, past and present, particularly its history and religious sociology, and his failure to take into consideration intra-cultural dynamics and differences. As a conscious rejoinder to Huntington's scheme, Richard Bulliet, a professor of Islamic history at Columbia University, coined the term "Islamo-Christian civilization" to underscore in particular the intellectual and epistemic commonalities that have historically existed between the two world civilizations.[9] Interestingly, in Muslim-majority societies, Huntington's Manichaean world-view resonates among hardline and radical Islamists, who similarly imagine a fundamental civilizational divide based on irreconcilable values and world-views.

Islamophobia has become even more entrenched and more widespread in the United States after the 2016 election of Donald J. Trump. Trump himself has been quoted as saying "Islam hates us," personifying Islam as a hate-spewing organism. Rhetoric of this sort has helped to galvanize nativist and xenophobic political opposition to American Muslims in an unprecedented way. Inflammatory rhetoric circulating on the internet and the popular media and increasingly purveyed by government officials and members of Congress have led to a spike in violence against American Muslims. According to the Southern Poverty Law Centre, which tracks extremism in the United States, the number of hate groups active in the United States have continued to rise since 2016, propelled in part by the mainstreaming of far-right rhetoric by the Trump presidency, particularly on topics like immigration and Islam. The number of anti-Muslim groups grew the most, almost tripling to 101 in 2016 from 34 in 2015. In the first 10 days alone after Trump's election, the centre said, it documented 867 bias incidents, including more than 300 that targeted immigrants or Muslims. Anti-Islamic hatemongering is also the province of certain powerful "think tanks" in the US who attempt to whip up public paranoia about "creeping Sharia" and about an assumed worldwide Muslim conspiracy to take over the West.[10]

Outside of the United States, Islamophobia rages in other Western societies. On July 22, 2011, a 32-year old Norwegian man by the name of Anders Breivik planted a bomb in an Oslo government building that caused eight fatalities. At his court arraignment a few days later in Oslo, Breivik admitted to his crimes and declared that his violence was motivated by a desire to rid Europe of Muslims and thereby destroy what he claimed was an "ongoing Islamic colonization of Europe."[11] He claimed to be influenced by the inflammatory rhetoric of Dutch politician and provocateur Geert Wilders, who regularly inveighs against the Muslim presence in Europe, and by the books of the American journalist Bruce Bawer, who lives in Norway and writes incendiary tracts against Muslims. In France, Muslims in visible religious attire – particularly women in *hijab* – are routinely harassed and legally prosecuted. The construction of *minarets* (prayer towers of mosques) have been banned in Switzerland and *halal* (and *kosher*) meat have been banned in Belgium. In a more distant part of the world, in March 2019, the Al-Noor mosque and Linwood Islamic Centre in Christchurch, New Zealand were attacked by an Australian white nationalist, Brenton Harrison Tarrant, during which more than 50 people were killed and many others injured.

To combat this scourge of Islamophobia, American Muslim advocacy and civil rights groups are spearheading efforts to push back against anti-

Islamic rhetoric and policies and allow Muslims to represent themselves in all their diversity. Among such organizations are the Council on American-Islamic Relations (CAIR), the Muslim Public Action Committee (MPAC), the Islamic Society of North America (ISNA), and the Islamic Council of North America (ICNA), which regularly hold conferences, workshops, and information sessions to challenge Islamophobia, provide representation for Muslim citizens in the political and civil spheres, and advocate for the civil and human rights of American Muslims in myriad ways. These organizations furthermore perform outreach to other religious communities and participate in interfaith activities in order to promote religious and political freedom and combat bigotry. They liaise with members of churches, synagogues, and other houses of worship and have established broad coalitions with ethnic and special interest groups representing, for example, Americans of Japanese, Sikh, and Hindu backgrounds – all of whom have similarly encountered cultural ostracism, racism, and violence specifically directed at them in American society. American Muslim groups also work hand-in-hand with secular civil rights and legal advocacy groups, such as the American Civil Liberties Union (ACLU), the Southern Poverty Law Centre, the American Bar Association, and others to defend their rights as American citizens.

Radicalism is not a problem uniquely confronting Muslims, of course; all religious communities are grappling with some version of it in the context of secular modernity. This recognition has propelled a number of mainstream Christian groups in particular to forge alliances with Muslim groups in the United States. Such mainstream Christian groups are appalled by their rightwing co-religionists, who indiscriminately malign Islam and Muslims. They seek instead to build bridges with Muslims on the basis of a shared understanding of the human relation to the divine and commonly-held values of compassion, charity, and concern for social justice. Among such notable initiatives is the Interfaith Alliance, composed of several Christian churches, Muslim organizations, and secular groups, that has recently redoubled its efforts to combat religious bigotry and promote religious freedom for all.

One of the newest and most effective initiatives to combat Islamophobia has been launched by the Alwaleed bin Talal Centre for Muslim-Christian Understanding at Georgetown University in Washington, D.C. Called the

Bridge Initiative, this initiative seeks "to expose—and marginalize—the influence of the individuals and groups who make up the Islamophobia network in America by actively working to divide Americans against one another through misinformation..."[12] The initiative puts out a daily bulletin which provides information about Islamophobic incidents in different parts of the world. Shockingly, they never run out of news items to report on this critical and depressing topic.

IV Dare We Be Hopeful?
Despite the horrifying trends outlined above, I am buoyed by the increasing efforts of common citizens in different parts of the globe to resist and combat hatred and bigotry in all its forms. I think of the first Muslim ban imposed by the Trump administration which prohibited the entry of visitors and immigrants from a number of Muslim-majority countries. Ordinary Americans – all descendants of immigrants themselves – showed their outrage over this discriminatory ban by flocking spontaneously to major airports and staging impromptu protests against the administration. Since then, people of good will all over the world continue to band together to oppose rabid nationalism and their pernicious consequences, wherever they may be found. Their combined efforts augur well specifically for relations between Christians and Muslims in the long run, the two largest religious groups in the world today.

Am I an incorrigible optimist? I do not think so. Like Christians, Muslims are expected to have hope. Giving into despair (*ya's* in Arabic) is a moral and spiritual failing (Qur'an 39:53). A Muslim's belief in an utterly good, compassionate, and just Supreme Being who repeatedly forgives human weakness and sin should be a shield against the loss of hope. Our faith – however imperfect, fragile, and flawed -- always offers the promise that all things that lead to justice, beauty, and mercy are possible with God and in peaceful cooperation with His created beings.

Notes

1. Asma Afsaruddin, "The Hermeneutics of Inter-Faith Relations: Retrieving Moderation and Pluralism as Universal Principles in Qur'anic Exegeses," in *Journal of Religious Ethics* 37 (2009): 331-54.
2. Ibid.
3. Al-Tabari, *Jami' al-bayan fi ta'wil al-qur'an*, Beirut: Dar al-kutub al-'ilmiyya, 1997, 11:398.
4. The full text of *A Common Word between Us and You*, is available at https://www.acommonword.com/downloads/CW-Booklet-Final-v6_8-1-09.pdf
5. For this discussion, see Asma Afsaruddin, "Discerning a Qur'anic Mandate for Mutually Transformational Dialogue," in Catherine Cornille, (ed.), Criteria of Discernment in Interreligious Dialogue, Eugene: Wipf & Stock, 2009, 101-121.
6. "Loving God and Neighbour Together: A Christian Response to 'A Common Word between Us and You'," *New York Times*, November 18, 2007
7. Richard Dawkins, *The God Delusion*, New York: Houghton Mifflin Harcourt, 2006, 232.
8. Samuel Huntington, "The Clash of Civilizations?" Foreign Affairs 72 (1993): 22–49; idem, *The Clash of Civilizations and the Remaking of World Order*, New York: Simon and Schuster, 1996.
9. Richard Bulliet, *The Case for an Islamo-Christian Civilization*, New York: Columbia University Press, 2006.
10. Wajahat Ali, Eli Clifton, Matthew Duss, Lee Fang, Scott Keyes, and Faiz Shakir, *Fear, Inc. The Roots of the Islamophobia Network in America* (August 2011), 2-3; available at: https://cdn.americanprogress.org/wp-content/uploads/issues/2011/08/pdf/islamophobia_intro.pdf
11. Ibid., 1.
12. Their website can be accessed at: https://bridge.georgetown.edu/

Part Five: Theological Forum - Public Theology in the Digital Age

Who Participates in the Digital Theological Conversation?

STEPHEN OKEY

To make sense of theology as a public discipline in the contemporary world, theologies must reckon with the digital context that shapes much of public conversation. As argued by Sherry Turkle and Stig Hjarvard, digital communications technologies increasingly mediate both the personal and communal, and so their design have an impact on human practices and attitudes. As a result, theology must critically consider the ambiguous effects of the digital on who participates in public conversation, the insularity of communities of conversation, and the spiritual disciplines that undergird theological conversation.

Discussions of public theology often take one of two approaches. First are what one might call a "theology of the public sphere," which seeks to reckon with the theological relevance of the public and sometimes the political realm of human affairs.[1] Second are what one might call "public acts of theology," where theological conversations are held in public spaces beyond the academic or ecclesial contexts that birthed them.[2] In a recent essay, Nichole M. Flores takes up both approaches, arguing that a wide range of public spaces need greater engagement from theologians.[3] Noting the greater diversity of persons engaged in theology and spaces where theology might happen, Flores calls for "theology to engage its publics in new, embodied, creative and faithful ways."[4]

The need for public theology to be embodied, creative, and faithful is nowhere more evident than in the digital world. The pervasiveness, accessibility, and convenience of digital technology has made the burgeoning digital sphere into an expansive public realm for theological engagement. Yet as important as it is for theologians to enter into this sphere, public theology must also reckon with how the design of these technologies and the attitudes and practices they engender can shape such public theological conversation. In order to understand what public theology in digital culture looks like, this brief essay looks at the work of Sherry Turkle and Stig Hjarvard. Drawing on their claims that digital technology has become an essential medium for interpersonal and communal conversation, it argues that digital technology makes for an ambiguous context for public theology. The gifts that it offers come with their own perils, which theologians must engage critically and carefully.

I Digital Reshaping of the Publics:
In her 2012 text *Alone Together*, Sherry Turkle claims that "technology proposes itself as the architect of our intimacies."[5] Devices, especially computers and cellphones, have created new layers of mediation that configure and filter human interaction, which lead people to view one another as "objects to be accessed" for one's own satisfaction without regard to the needs or challenges of the other.[6] The mobility of such technology enables constant connection while hindering opportunities for disconnection, privacy, and self-reflection.[7] New communications technologies have thus enabled people to "enjoy continual connection but rarely have each other's full attention."[8]

In her more recent book *Reclaiming Conversation*, she uses Henry David Thoreau's "three chairs" image to structure her analysis of the difficulties that many today find with conversation.[9] The so-called "flight from conversation" that she diagnoses has not only made solitude harder to find and reframed how people think of friendship; it has profoundly shaped the way people participate in public conversation. She notes the danger of echo chambers, the rise of (self) surveillance, and the persistent sense of emergency that have all been engendered by pervasive digital technology as challenges to thoughtful public conversation.[10]

The idea that digital communications technology would reshape public discourse is part of what Stig Hjarvard calls mediatization. He defines mediatization as the process through which

"the media have developed into an independent institution in society and, as a consequence, other institutions have become increasingly dependent on the media and have to accommodate the logic of the media in order to be able to communicate with other institutions and society as a whole."[11]

This process is increasingly a facet of the Western social context akin to other "meta-processes" like globalization and secularization.[12] Its effects may be felt in a wide range of institutions, including governments, corporations, and not-for-profits.

Mediatization is partly a result of rapid technological development in media. Hjarvard notes two major impacts from this shift: first, media devices like TVs and smartphones have made media more accessible and affordable, making media engagement significantly more widespread and persistent. Like Turkle, Hjarvard argues that interpersonal interaction is increasingly mediated and filtered through such devices.[13] Second, the corporate structures for monetizing and commodifying the content and the forms of media have developed as well (think especially here of the evolution of advertising from the mid-19th century to today).[14]

Of primary interest to Hjarvard is how these changes have impacted religion. He describes mediatization as a possible "theoretical framework for the understanding of how media work as agents of religious change."[15] The principal change wrought by mediatization has been that "the media have taken over many of the social functions that used to be performed by religious institutions."[16] As a result, media has become the dominant institution with and through which most people interact. This is true in Turkle's sense of the "architect of our intimacies," but also in terms of many of the narratives and content that people use to engage fundamental questions of meaning.

For example, Hjarvard claims that while religious communities had typically been the primary producers of religious content, the process of mediatization has led to such sources increasingly being "produced and edited by the media and delivered through genres like news, documentaries, drama, comedy, [and] entertainment."[17] The genre of such content is more and more that of "pop culture," which he describes as influential because it orients its content towards "entertainment and the consumer." This engenders an individualistic approach to religion more concerned with personal satisfactions than communal commitments.[18]

Because of these kinds of changes, Hjarvard argues that religion not only has lost its dominance in creating and defining symbols and meaning but has also become dependent on the media to convey those symbols and meaning at all. Religious and secular symbols now compete with one another in the media through the same formats and structures. Indeed, he claims that the institution of the media encompasses, perhaps even surpasses, religious institutions, such that the religious institutions are forced to depend on media institutions and thus to cede a growing degree of authority over their symbols and meanings.

II Digital Impact on the Public Practice of Theology

According to both Turkle and Hjarvard, digital communications media are increasingly the context in which private and public conversation occur. The design of the technologies enables them to exercise significant influence on interpersonal and communal relations, which in turn affects how persons perceive what is public and how they engage that. From Turkle and Hjarvard's work, three essential insights into the digital sphere as public emerge.

First, digital culture has enabled a wider range of persons to engage in public theological conversation. This is best evidenced by platforms like social media and blogging, which have made it possible for voices that previously did not have access to traditional platforms for public discussion (e.g. mainstream media) to develop such platforms on their own. However, by lowering the barriers to entry, digital culture has also exacerbated the devaluation of expertise. One can find online whatever advice, information, or wisdom one seeks, including those that will confirm one's preexisting biases. Whenever one encounters a so-called "expert" with whom one disagrees, they can be easily dismissed and replaced by one closer to one's views.

Second, the digital sphere has improved the possibilities for niche communities to grow despite physical and geographic separation. This effect was evident already by the late 1990s, as Heidi Campbell showed in her research on listserv-based spiritual communities.[19] Digital technology has enabled communities like "Weird Catholic Twitter"[20] or the Zen Buddhism subreddit to grow and provide forums for public theological engagement and conversation.

However, the ability to form niche communities comes also with the possibility of limiting oneself to membership in like-minded groups. Referred to sometimes as silos or echo chambers, digital technology can make it easy to filter out a range of view, either intentionally or not. While there remains significant debate as to whether social media is contributing to social polarization via such echo chambers, there is good evidence that digital technology can contribute to "prejudice reinforcement."[21]

Third, digital culture has made it more difficult to develop the sort of spiritual disciplines that enable public theological conversation, particularly regarding contemplation and authenticity. This is partly due to the success of digital technology at drawing and sustaining a person's attention, often to the point of consistent distraction. It is also due to the strongly performative aspect of how people present themselves online, which is often more about signalling that one is a certain type of person (whether true or not) than it is about authentically being the type of person one truly is. Such challenges to contemplation and authenticity can undermine the practice of public theology precisely because they push against a participant's opportunity for thoughtful, intentional giving of oneself to public conversation.

III Conclusion

Digital culture is indeed one of the many publics that Flores calls for theologians to engage more creatively and faithfully. However, it is also one that carries particular challenges for theologians, thanks to the design of digital technologies and the attendant attitudes and practices that they inculcate in their participants. If there is to be a bright future for digital, public theology, it must discern how best to engage digital culture without simply being subsumed into it.

Notes

1. See, for example, David Tracy, *The Analogical Imagination: Christian Theology and the Culture of Pluralism*, New York: Crossroad, 1981 and Charles T. Mathewes, *A Theology of Public Life*, Cambridge: Cambridge University Press, 2008.
2. Consider here the mid-20th century work of Martin Luther King, Jr, Reinhold Niebuhr, and John Courtney Murray, SJ in the United States. More recently, one might look to

public debates like those between Massimo Faggioli and Ross Douthat (Peter Feuerhard, "Faggioli, Douthat Discuss Francis' First Five Years," *National Catholic Reporter*, 2 February 2018, at https://www.ncronline.org/news/people/faggioli-douthat-discuss-francis-first-five-years [12 December 2019]).
3. Nichole M. Flores, "What Is the Role of a Public Theologian Today?" *America Magazine*, 22 July 2019, at https://www.americamagazine.org/arts-culture/2019/07/12/what-role-public-theologian-today [12 December 2019].
4. Flores, "What is the Role of a Public Theologian Today?"
5. Sherry Turkle, *Alone Together: Why We Expect More from Technology and Less from Each Other*, New York: Basic Books, 2011, 1.
6. Turkle, *Alone Together*, 154
7. Turkle, *Alone Together*, 177, 203
8. Turkle, *Alone Together*, 280
9. "I had three chairs in my house: one for solitude, two for friendship, three for society." Henry David Thoreau, quoted in Sherry Turkle, *Reclaiming Conversation: The Power of Talk in a Digital Age*, New York: Penguin Books, 2016, x, 46-50.
10. Turkle, *Reclaiming Conversation*, 293-316
11. Stig Hjarvard, "The Mediatization of Religion: A Theory of the Media as Agents of Religious Change," *Northern Lights* 6.1 (2008), 9-26, here 11.
12. Hjarvard, "The Mediatization of Religion," 10
13. Hjarvard, "The Mediatization of Religion," 13
14. Hjarvard, "The Mediatization of Religion," 16
15. Hjarvard, "The Mediatization of Religion," 11
16. Hjarvard, "The Mediatization of Religion," 10
17. Hjarvard, "The Mediatization of Religion," 12
18. Hjarvard, "The Mediatization of Religion," 12-13
19. Heidi Campbell, *Exploring Religious Community Online: We Are One in the Network*, New York: Peter Lang, 2005.
20. Mary Meisenzahl, "Inside the World of Weird Catholic Twitter — and the 'Rad Trads' Keeping the Old Traditions Alive," *MEL Magazine*, 10 March 2019, at https://melmagazine.com/en-us/story/rad-trad-weird-catholic-twitter [8 December 2019].
21. Amol Rajan, "Do Digital Echo Chambers Exist?," *BBC News*, 4 March 2019, at https://www.bbc.com/news/entertainment-arts-47447633 [6 December 2019].

Millennials and Public Theology in a Digital Age

KATHERINE G. SCHMIDT

Millennial theologians engage in theological reflection with a unique awareness of the effects of digital culture on the theological project. This alters both their methodologies as well as their objects of study, expanding the theological reflection in the digital age to include the doctrinal ramifications of form as well as content.

"Millennials" are no longer the students about whom faculty and administrators worry. They are now junior and not so junior colleagues, writing and teaching a whole new generation of college students. Yet generational differences are real, and as American political, economic, and social life finds itself in real turmoil, these differences do shape both individual and communal values.

Younger theologians have been steeped in the tradition of contextual theology. Therefore, it comes somewhat naturally to millennial theologians to consider the way(s) in which generational differences affect the subjects and methods of their work. I am myself a millennial theologian. From this vantage point, I submit that no other context has had a greater effect on academic and pastoral theology in the American context in the past decade than the digital, with the possible and growing exception of the climate crisis.[1] Digital culture has changed both "how" and "where" of theology in meaningful but challenging ways. For most theologians, the change has come mostly in the "where" of theology, as digital fora have dramatically altered theological discourse. To the extent that social, economic, political, and academic life is reliant upon digital apparatuses, theology is being constantly shaped by digital culture.

I The "How" of Theology in a Digital Age

Theologians pursue their work in reliance on digital platforms. They come to their research subjects in various ways, but we are hard pressed to find scholars arriving at their topics without some influence of digital culture. I want to begin with a basic point: digital technology has changed the social imaginary. According to Charles Taylor, the social imaginary is "an incorporating sense of the normal expectations we have of each other."[2] Digital logics are changing social expectations, but they are also changing the meaning of basic notions such as "social" and "human."

Doing theology in the digital age, then, means that to the extent that theologians care at all about what it means to be human and human-together (social), their subjects are being shaped by the dynamics of digital culture. We both shape and are shaped by the wide variety of forms through which we mean to encounter nature, God, and one another.

Perhaps the best analogy here is language; digital culture requires that we learn the language of its discourse. As much as knowing this language (and practicing it regularly) opens new opportunities for research, it is another matrix through which sources, including Revelation, must pass. Ironically, in our persistent desire for more access to reality—historical, natural, and theological—we embed ourselves in more and more layers of mediation of which we must be conscious as we do our work.[3]

Beyond awareness of the digital-cultural matrix, millennial theology seeks sometimes surprising sources for its theological reflection. It is not unlike the various turns in academic theology to the social question, to lived experiences of marginalized people, or to political life in the modern world. Theological reflection is ever bound to history, laying before theologians the human realities upon which the Revelation of God is to be brought to bear. Therefore, more and more millennial theologians are mining the experience of digital culture—in all its absurdity and perplexity—for possible theological reflection.

II The "Where" of Theology in a Digital Age

Since the 1990s at least, internet theorists have championed the democratizing effect of digital space, and much of the early optimism about the internet's possibilities has proven justified. But in the wake of the election of Donald Trump, there has been much research about the role of internet communities in the resurgence of extreme right-wing groups across the globe. For the Church, this resurgence seems to have, at the very least, perpetuated a divisive and caustic *modus operandi* online that threatens to usher in a new era of schism. A brief perusal of so-called "Catholic twitter" will bear this out in short order.

These digital spaces are legion and unregulated, featuring a tidal wave of theological commentary from all kinds of interested parties, regardless of theological training. This kind of vast participation comes mostly from laity but is often encouraged and informally sponsored by clerical leaders as well, also of variant (and sometime dubious) theological training. At first blush, this kind of lay participation seems to be the fruition of some of Vatican II's dreams for the Church, but one wonders exactly how the Church will survive the deluge of ideological in-fighting devoid of theological boundary.

One of the issues facing the Church in this age is the notion of public theology itself. Digital theology disrupts the very category of public to the extent that it introduces new semi-public and semi-private spaces for community and individual identity. Furthermore, what qualifies as "theology" is also up for debate online, though standards do persist in both academic and formally ecclesial circles. To what extent do these standards matter to the majority of Catholics, if so many of them are imbibing theological ideas from unregulated online sources?[3] Trained theologians and ordained ministers wring their hands and demand some appeal to authority, and the bloggers blog on, largely unaffected.

III *Exempli Gratia*

A recent controversy offers a helpful example for considering what I have suggested above. When two men took it upon themselves to throw pieces of artworks into the Tiber, they did so squarely in the context of the "digital age." A four-minute video entitled "Pachamama idols thrown into the Tiber river!" appeared on YouTube in October of 2019. The video is actually a compilation of videos shot during the same event, namely the stealing of recently-blessed statues of naked Amazonian women from the Santa Maria Church in Rome. The video's climax shows a man, later revealed to be Austrian lay Catholic Alexander Tschugguel, setting the three wooden statues on the mantle of the bridge and dramatically knocking them into the Tiber River.

The video unsurprisingly set off a firestorm of the Catholic world, especially online. But not enough has been said from a theological perspective about the medium of this story, the YouTube video itself. Tschugguel's choice is somewhat intuitive here: a YouTube video would be an incredibly effective means by which to show the world this symbolic act. Yet the choice is also deeply contradictory of Tschugguel's own intentions.

While the statues' dramatic descent into the river does mark the video's climax, the videographer makes a very important choice around the 2:20 mark: he pans the camera up to the Castel Sant'Angelo. The iconic cylindrical building features prominently as an imposing foil for the act of defiance to come. Regular users of video-based social media like Instagram or Snapchat know intuitively that panning in this way is not accidental. It is concerted and often meaningful. One could make the case that taking the time to pan to the Castel was simply to give a point of geographical reference, but this seems unlikely given the highly symbolic nature of the act itself. More likely, the Castel represents Church leadership who blessed and placed the statues in the church in the first place, namely Pope Francis himself. Tschugguel later told National Catholic Register that he believes the Church is "not leading the way anymore, but following the world."[4]

If we focus too much on the doctrinal debate within the video, we miss the theological import of its chosen medium. In uploading his self-made, self-produced video, Tschugguel compounds his act of defiance, circumventing church structures for his ideological claim, just as he did in the choice to steal the statues itself. In his self-proclaimed efforts to defend Catholic doctrine he thus decided to pursue the most Protestant of paths: utilizing the media of his time to openly defy the Church and its pope, stoking the embers of schism in the name of catholicity.

To consider media as theologically weighted is the onus of theologians in the digital age. This is especially true of those of us theologians who carry the formative experiences of digital culture with us by virtue of our age. The ways in which our lives have become enmeshed in virtual spaces have altered our notions of what it means to be human and what it means to be human together. This means that our lives online are fertile ground for theological reflection, however complicated they prove to be.

Notes

1. Elsewhere, I have argued that the digital subsumes the logics of globalized capitalism, which offers itself as truly the dominant context for all theological work in the 21st century.
2. Charles Taylor, *A Secular Age*, Cambridge: Harvard University Press, 2007, 172.
3. See Bolter and Grusin, *Remediation: Understanding New Media*, Cambridge: MIT Press, 2000.
4. The now defunct Pontifical Council on Social Communications saw this problem early, when in 2000 they wrote, "A special aspect of the Internet, as we have seen, concerns the sometimes confusing proliferation of unofficial web sites labeled 'Catholic'." *The Church and Internet*, 11.
5. Edward Pentin, "Austrian Catholic: Why I Threw Pachamama Statues into the Tiber," *National Catholic Register* (November 4, 2019).

Contributors

DR WILHELMUS G.B.M. (PIM) VALKENBERG studied theology and religious studies in the Netherlands where he worked at Radboud University Nijmegen for twenty years before continuing his teaching and research in the United States. At present, he is a professor of Religion and Culture at the Catholic University of America in Washington D.C. His main interests are in Comparative Theology, Interreligious Dialogue, and Christian – Muslim Relations.
Address: 4911 Crowson Avenue, Baltimore MD 21212, USA
Email: valkenberg@cua.edu

VEBJØRN L. HORSFJORD is professor of religious studies at Inland Norway University of Applied Sciences. He is the author of *Common Words in Muslim-Christian Dialogue. A Study of Texts from the Common Word Dialogue Process* (Brill Rodopi, 2018). He has published on interreligious relations and the Orthodox tradition and human rights, as well as books on interreligious cooperation and on global Christianity in Norwegian.
Address: Inland Norway University of Applied Sciences, PO Box 400, 2418 Elverum, Norway
Email: vebjorn.horsfjord@inn.no

JOSHUA RALSTON is a Reader in Christian-Muslim Relations at the University of Edinburgh and founder and director of the Christian-Muslim Studies Network. He is the author of *Law and the Rule of God: A Christian Engagement with Shari'a* and has published numerous essays and book chapters on Protestant theology, Christian-Muslim dialogue, and political theology.
Address: New College, Mound Place, Edinburgh EH1 2LX, UK
Email: joshua.ralston@ed.ac.uk

Contributors

WILLIAM SKUDLAREK, a monk of Saint John's Abbey in Collegeville, Minnesota, is Secretary General of Dialogue Interreligieux Monastique·Monastic Interreligious Dialogue (DIM·MID) and managing editor of its on-line journal Dilatato Corde. He is the author of *Demythologizing Celibacy: Practical Wisdom from Christian and Buddhist Monasticism* (Collegeville MN: Liturgical Press, 2008) and the editor and/or translator of several books in the area of monastic interreligious dialogue.
  Address: Saint John's Abbey, Box 2015, Collegeville MN, USA
  Email: wskudlarek@csbsju.edu

CHRISTIAN KROKUS is associate professor and chair of the department of theology/religious studies at the University of Scranton, a Catholic and Jesuit university, where his teaching and research focus on Christian-Muslim comparative theology. He is the author of *The Theology of Louis Massignon: Islam, Christ, and the Church* (CUA, 2017).
  Address: Department of Theology/Religious Studies, University of Scranton, 800 Linden Street, Scranton, PA 18510, USA
  Email: christian.krokus@scranton.edu

ALBERTUS BAGUS LAKSANA, S.J., is currently dean of Sanata Dharma University School of Theology in Yogyakarta, Indonesia. He received his PhD in comparative theology from Boston College (2011) with a focus on Muslim-Christian encounters. He previously taught at Loyola Marymount University, Los Angeles. His area of research covers both Catholic systematic theology and the intersections between theology and culture, Asian theologies, comparative theology and theology of religions. His publications include *Muslim and Catholic Pilgrimage Practices: Explorations through Java* (Routledge 2014) and essays in different journals such as *The International Journal of Asian Christianity* and *Kritika Kultura*.
  Address: Albertus Bagus Laksana, S.J., Dean of the School of Theology, Sanata Dharma University. Jl. Kaliurang, Kayen, Condongcatur, Kec. Depok, Kabupaten Sleman, Daerah Istimewa Yogyakarta 55281, Indonesia
  Email: bagus.laksana@gmail.com

Contributors

KLAUS VON STOSCH is Professor of Catholic Systematic Theology and head of the centre for comparative theology and cultural studies at the university of Paderborn. Recent publications include *The other Prophet. Jesus in the Qur'an* (together with Mouhanad Khorchide, London: Gingko, 2019) *Herausforderung Islam. Christliche Annäherungen* (third edition, Paderborn: Ferdinand Schöningh, 2018), *Einführung in die Systematische Theologie* (fourth edition, Paderborn: utb 2018).
    Address: Prof. Dr. Klaus von Stosch, Universität Paderborn, Fakultät für Kulturwissenschaften, Warburger Str. 100/ N3.146, D – 33098 Paderborn, Germandy
    Email: Klaus.von.stosch@uni-paderborn.de

LAURIE JOHNSTON is Associate Professor of Theology at Emmanuel College, Boston. She holds degrees from Harvard Divinity School and Boston College. She is the editor, with Jay Carney, of *The Surprise of Reconciliation in the Catholic Tradition* (2018), and editor, with Tobias Winright, of *Can War Be Just in the Twenty-first Century* (2015). During 2018 she was a visiting Fulbright Scholar at the Katholieke Universiteit Leuven, Belgium.
    Address: Dr. Laurie Johnston, Department of Theology and Religious Studies, Emmanuel College, 400 Fenway, Boston, MA 02115, USA
    Email: johnsla@emmanuel.edu

CLAUDIO MONGE is head of the DoSt-I (Dominican Study – Istanbul), the cultural centre of the Dominicans in Istanbul. A Doctor in Theology of Religions and Invited Professor at the University of Fribourg (Switzerland) and at the ISE in Venice. He is the author of *Dieu hôte. Enquête sur l'hospitalité en histoire et en théologie comparées des religions à la lumière de Gn.18* (Bucarest: Zetabooks: 2008), *Stranieri con Dio* (Milan: Terrasanta, 2013), and a number of important articles on the theology of dialogue and interreligious hospitality, including the recent 'Le risque fou de l'hospitalité. De l'étrangéité ontologique à l'étrangéité théologique', *Théologiques*, vol. 25/2 (2017), 37-60 and 'Nominare l'Ineffabile: il problema del nome di dio nei testi sacri delle religioni abramitiche', *Sacra Doctrina*, Vol.64/1 (2019), 184-213.
    Address: DoSt-I (Dominican Study - Istanbul), Sen Piyer Kilisesi,

Contributors

alata Kulesi sok. 26 Bereketzade mah., TK - 34420 Karaköy – ISTANBUL, Turkey.
 Email: galatacla@gmail.com

MARINUS CHIJIOKE IWUCHUKWU, an Associate Professor and chair of Theology Department at Duquesne University. The title of his last book is: *Muslim-Christian Dialogue in Postcolonial Northern Nigeria: The Challenges of Inclusive Cultural and Religious Pluralism*. He is also the current chair of the Consortium for Christian-Muslim Dialogue at Duquesne University.
 Address: Marinus C. Iwuchukwu, PhD, Duquesne University, Theology Department – Fisher Hall 602, 600 Forbes Ave, Pittsburgh, PA 15282, USA
 Address 2: 1 Thorncrest Dr., Pittsburgh, PA 15235, USA
 Email: iwuchukwum@duq.edu

JEAN DRUEL is a French Dominican friar. He lives in Cairo. Since October 2014, he is director of the Dominican Institute for Oriental Studies (IDEO). After a Master's Degree in theology and Coptic patrology (*L'expérience spirituelle de saint Pachôme...*, Catholic Institute in Paris, 2002), he obtained a degree in Teaching Arabic as Foreign Language (*Emphatic sounds in educated Cairene Arabic*, American University in Cairo, 2006). In 2012, he completed a PhD thesis in the history of Arabic grammar under the supervision of Pr. Kees Versteegh (*Numerals in Arabic grammatical theory*, Nijmegen University). He currently studies an unedited manuscript of Sībawayh's (d. 180/796?) *Kitāb* in Arabic grammar.
 Address: Dominican Institute for Oriental Studies, 1, al-Tarabishi Street, 11831 Cairo, Egypt
 Email: jean.druel@ideo-cairo.org

DANIEL A. MADIGAN, S.J., is Ruesch Family Distinguished Jesuit Scholar at Georgetown University, Director of Graduate Studies in the Department of Theology and Religious Studies, Senior Fellow of the Al-Waleed Centre for Muslim-Christian Understanding, and Faculty Fellow of the Berkley Centre for Religion, Peace and World Affairs. He is also an Honorary Professorial Fellow of Australian Catholic University. In 2012 he became Chair of the Building Bridges Seminar, an annual five-day study session for Muslim and Christian scholars invited from all over the world.

Address: Ruesch Family Associate Professor, Director of Graduate Studies, Dept. of Theology and Religious Studies, 139 New North, Georgetown University, Washington DC 20057, USA

Email: dam76@georgetown.edu

ASMA AFSARUDDIN is a professor of Islamic Studies at Indiana University, Bloomington, USA. She is the author or editor of seven books, including *Contemporary Issues in Islam* (Edinburgh University Press, 2015) and *Striving in the Path of God: Jihad and Martyrdom in Islamic Thought* (Oxford University Press, 2013), for which she received grants from the Harry Frank Guggenheim Foundation and the Carnegie Corporation of New York.. She is currently a member of the academic council of the Alwaleed Centre for Muslim-Christian Understanding at Georgetown University and a past member of the Board of Directors of the American Academy of Religion.

Address: Hamilton Lugar School 3041, Indiana University, 355 N. Jordan Avenue, Bloomington, IN 47405, USA

Email: aafsarud@indiana.edu

STEPHEN OKEY is an Associate Professor of Theology at Saint Leo University, where he teaches courses in systematic theology and ethics. He is the author of *A Theology of Conversation: An Introduction to David Tracy.*

Address: University Campus – MC2127, PO Box 6665, Saint Leo, FL 33574-6665, USA

Email: Stephen.okey@saintleo.edu

KATHERINE G. SCHMIDT is Assistant Professor of Theology and Religious Studies at Molloy College in Rockville Centre, NY.

Address: 84-50 Austin Street, Apt. 3G, Kew Gardens, NY 11415, USA

Email: kschmidt@molloy.edu

CONCILIUM
International Journal of Theology

FOUNDERS
Anton van den Boogaard; Paul Brand; Yves Congar, OP; Hans Küng;
Johann Baptist Metz; Karl Rahner, SJ; Edward Schillebeeckx

BOARD OF DIRECTORS
President: Thierry-Marie Courau OP
Vice-Presidents: Linda Hogan and Daniel Franklin Pilario CM

BOARD OF EDITORS
Susan Abraham, Los Angeles (USA)
Michel Andraos, Chicago (USA)
Mile Babic´ OFM, Sarajevo (Bosna i Hercegovina)
Antony John Baptist, Bangalore (India)
Michelle Becka, Würzburg (Deutschland)
Bernadeth Caero Bustillos, Osnabrück (Deutschland)
Catherine Cornille, Boston (USA)
Thierry-Marie Courau OP, Paris (France)
Geraldo Luiz De Mori SJ, Belo Horizonte (Brasil)
Enrico Galavotti, Chieti (Italia)
Margareta Gruber OSF, Vallendar (Deutschland)
Linda Hogan, Dublin (Ireland)
Huang Po-Ho, Tainan (Zhōnghuá Mínguó)
Stefanie Knauss, Villanova (USA)
Carlos Mendoza-Álvarez OP, Ciudad de México (México)
Gianluca Montaldi FN, Brescia (Italia)
Agbonkhianmeghe Orobator SJ, Nairobi (Kenya)
Daniel Franklin Pilario CM, Quezon City (Filipinas)
Léonard Santedi Kinkupu, Kinshasa (RD Congo)
João J. Vila-Chã SJ, Roma (Italia)

PUBLISHERS
SCM Press (London, UK)
Matthias-Grünewald Verlag (Ostfildern, Germany)
Editrice Queriniana (Brescia, Italy)
Editorial Verbo Divino (Estella, Spain)
EditoraVozes (Petropolis, Brazil)

Concilium Secretariat:
Couvent de l'Annonciation
222 rue du Faubourg Saint-Honoré
75008 – Paris (France)
secretariat.concilium@gmail.com
Executive secretary: Gianluca Montaldi FN

http://www.concilium.in

The Canterbury Dictionary of HYMNOLOGY   The result of over ten years of research by an international team of editors, The Canterbury Dictionary of Hymnology is the major online reference work on hymns, hymn-writers and traditions.

www.hymnology.co.uk

CHURCH TIMES   The Church Times, founded in 1863, has become the world's leading Anglican newspaper. It offers professional reporting of UK and international church news, in-depth features on faith, arts and culture, wide-ranging comment and all the latest clergy jobs. Available in print and online.

www.churchtimes.co.uk

Crucible   Crucible is the Christian journal of social ethics. It is produced quarterly, pulling together some of the best practitioners, thinkers, and theologians in the field. Each issue reflects theologically on a key theme of political, social, cultural, or environmental significance.

www.cruciblejournal.co.uk

JLS   Joint Liturgical Studies offers a valuable contribution to the study of liturgy. Each issue considers a particular aspect of liturgical development, such as the origins of the Roman rite, Anglican Orders, welcoming the Baptised, and Anglican Missals.

www.jointliturgicalstudies.co.uk

magnet   Magnet is a resource magazine published three times a year. Packed with ideas for worship, inspiring artwork and stories of faith and justice from around the world.

www.ourmagnet.co.uk

For more information on these publications visit the websites listed above or contact **Hymns Ancient & Modern:**
Tel.: +44 (0)1603 785 910
Write to: Subscriptions, Hymns Ancient & Modern,
13a Hellesdon Park Road, Norwich NR6 5DR

Concilium Subscription Information

December **2020/5:** *Differently Able: for a Church Where All Belong*

February **2021/1:** *Church and Theology at the Borders*

April **2021/2:** *Sinodalities*

July **2021/3**: *Incarnation in a Post/human Age*

October **2021/4:** *Amazonia - Gift and Task*

New subscribers: to receive the next five issues of Concilium *please copy this form, complete it in block capitals and send it with your payment to the address below. Alternatively subscribe online at www.conciliumjournal.co.uk*

Please enter my annual subscription for *Concilium* starting with issue 2020/5.

Individuals
____ £52 UK
____ £75 overseas and (Euro €92, US $110)

Institutions
____ £75 UK
____ £95 overseas and (Euro €120, US $145)

Postage included – airmail for overseas subscribers

Payment Details:
Payment can be made by cheque (£ Sterling only), by credit/debit card or bank transfer.
a. I enclose a cheque for £ _____ Payable to Hymns Ancient and Modern Ltd
b. To pay by Visa/Mastercard please contact us on +44(0)1603 785911 or go to www.conciliumjournal.co.uk
c. To pay in US $ or Euro € by bank transfer please contact us on +44(0)1603 785911

Contact Details:
Name ....
Address ....
....
Telephone .... E-mail ....

Send your order to *Concilium,* **Hymns Ancient and Modern Ltd**
13a Hellesdon Park Road, Norwich NR6 5DR, UK
E-mail: concilium@hymnsam.co.uk
or order online at www.conciliumjournal.co.uk

Customer service information
All orders must be prepaid. Your subscription will begin with the next issue of Concilium*. If you have any queries or require Information about other payment methods, please contact our Customer Services department.*

www.ingramcontent.com/pod-product-compliance
Ingram Content Group UK Ltd.
Pitfield, Milton Keynes, MK11 3LW, UK
UKHW042006230426
12048UKWH00009B/591

9 780334 059592